SEOUL
BOOK OF
Everything

Everything you wanted to know about
Seoul and were going to ask anyway

MACINTYRE PURCELL PUBLISHING INC.

TO OUR READERS

Every effort has been made by authors and editors to ensure that the information enclosed in this book is accurate and up-to-date. We revise and update annually, so if you discover any out-of-date or incorrect information, we would appreciate hearing from you at **info@bookofeverything.com**.

Copyright 2010 by MacIntyre Purcell Publishing Inc.

MacIntyre Purcell Publishing Inc.
232 Lincoln St., PO Box 1142
Lunenburg, Nova Scotia
B0J 2C0 Canada
www.bookofeverything.com
info@bookofeverything.com

Cover photo courtesy of the Seoul Tourism Organization
(representing Seoul Metropolitan Government)
Photos: Pages: 8, 24, 58, 72, 140, 196 Seoul Tourism Organization
Photos: Pages: 102, 122, 176, 218, 229 Istockphoto

Library and Archives Canada Cataloguing in Publication
Seoul book of everything : everything you wanted to know
about Seoul and were going to ask anyway / edited by Tim Lehnert.

ISBN 978-0-9810941-7-5
1. Seoul (Korea). 2. Seoul (Korea)--Miscellanea. I. Lehnert, Tim II. Title.

DS925.S44S45 2010   951.95   C2010-901172-4

Printed in Canada

Introduction

Like all great cities, Seoul is a product of its contradictions. It's an ancient city, with a legacy of having served as its nation's capital for over 600 years, yet it combines a reverence for the past with a full embrace of the future.

Seoul has led South Korea's rapid rise as an economic power and with that transformation has also come a flourishing in art, music, film and all aspects of design. The city is home to some of the world's most chic department stores and boutiques, but is also a place where you can buy ginseng and traditional clothing at a historic market in the city center. Seoul is the most wired metropolis on the planet, and launched the Korean Wave—the explosion of Korean pop culture worldwide in the 2000s—but remains a city where you can watch traditional drummers and dancers, or dine in the style of a Korean king from centuries ago. Seoul is an international city where you can just as easily immerse yourself in ancient Korean culture as enjoy an Italian-Asian fusion meal, or get your groove on at a hip-hop nightclub.

Seoul's mix of traditional and contemporary, local and international, eum and yang gives it a special flavor. It's a place of infinite possibilities and many stories. Its spectacular mountains have witnessed invasions, wars and occupations, yet also tremendous achievements in the arts, sciences, architecture, culture, education and technology.

Seoul is constantly evolving and reinventing itself. It's a city where there is always something going on: A newly launched street festival, the latest project from a superstar architect, or the renewal of an urban forest, river or plaza. Seoulites don't seem to rest. They work hard, play hard and approach everything from a meal out with friends to flying a kite with enthusiasm and passion.

Understanding, indeed grasping, a great city like Seoul can take a lifetime. What we have attempted to do here is capture lightning in a bottle, distill something of the essence of this dynamic place. The devil is in the details, and here the Han River, the palaces, the subway, the DMZ, Namdaemun and Dongdaemun markets, the 1988 Olympics and the Joseon Kingdom are covered, but so too are *jjimjilbang* (Korean saunas), Konglish (Korean English), heatwaves, kimchi, shamanism, K-Pop, *jaebeol*, the Chicken Art Museum and baseball Korean style.

The hardest part about compiling and writing a book on Seoul was deciding what not to include. It was an interesting ride. To help us get it right, we employed a team of Seoul-based writers, and asked a dozen other local experts for lists of five on topics ranging from mountains, tea houses, books and cultural treasures, to movies, night clubs and the weather.

Thanks to Robert Neff for his work on the "Then & Now," "Economy," "Politics" and "Urban Geography" chapters, Joel Levin for expert proofing, copy editing and the "Weather," Michael J. Meyers for "Language and Beliefs," Mary Crowe for "Food," and Tracey Stark and Daniel Gray for "Arts and Entertainment." Kim Young-sook's outstanding proofing and fact checking was also much appreciated. Thanks also to Don Kirk, Jennifer Flinn, Rob Ouwehand and Ann Kidder for their input.

Special thank-yous go out to our guest stars for generously providing lists of five. The insightful contributions of Choe Kwang-shik, Brother Anthony, Andrew Salmon, Lars Vargo, Mark Russell, David A. Mason, Richard Choi, Kim Seung-bai, Sam Hammington, Young-Iob Chung and Andrei Lankov are an essential part of the *Seoul Book of Everything*.

Thanks also to the Seoul Tourism Organization, in particular President and CEO Samuel Koo, as well as Maureen O'Crowley, Christina Song and Heayjin Lee. Finally, thanks to the City of Seoul and its people—working on this project has deepened my enthusiasm for one of the world's great cities.

Tim Lehnert on behalf of MacIntyre Purcell Publishing

Table of Contents

INTRODUCTION **4**

TIMELINE **9**

6,000 Years Ago to Present in 70 Points . . . The Joseon Kingdom . . .
King Sejong . . . Choe Kwang-shik's National Museum of Korea Treasures
. . .The Olympics and World Cup.

ESSENTIALS **25**

The Nitty Gritty . . . Comedian Sam Hammington's Things You Must
Bring to Korea . . . You Know You're From Seoul When . . . Iconic
Seoul . . . Royal Palaces . . . World Design Capital . . . Lars Vargo's
Top Korean Reads . . . Unique Meeting Venues . . . Super Convenient
Seoul . . . Medical Tourism . . . The DMZ . . . David A. Mason's Top
Seoul Mountains . . . Getting Around . . . Elite Universities.

WEATHER **59**

Korean Temperatures . . . Meteorologist Kim Seung-bai on Seoul's
Climate . . . Extreme Weather . . . Typhoons . . . Surviving Summer . . .
Climate Change . . . Highs and Lows . . . The Rainy Season.

URBAN GEOGRAPHY **73**

Geomantic Seoul . . . A Waterway Reborn . . . Gwanghwamun Square . . .
Namsan . . . Department Stores . . . To Market, to Market: Namdaemun,
Dongdaemun and More . . . Hanok . . . Odd Museums . . . Neighborhoods:
Itaewon, Insadong, Myeong-dong, Apgujeong and More . . . Living
Natural Monuments . . . Brother Anthony's Top Tea Houses . . . Best
Spots for the Changing Seasons . . . Han River . . . Green Spaces:
Olympic Park, Seoul Forest and More.

FOOD **103**

A Korean Food Primer . . . Five Classics . . . Celebratory Foods . . . Mind
Your Manners . . . Andrew Salmon's Top Places to Eat in Seoul . . .
Kimchi . . . Side Dishes . . . Mary Crowe's Top Korean Meals to Make at
Home . . . Royal Cuisine . . . Non-Korean Seoul Food . . . Street Eats . . .
Alcoholic Beverages and Snacks.

LANGUAGE AND BELIEFS **123**

The Korean Language . . . Hangeul . . . Essential Expressions . . . Names
and Nicknames . . . Idioms . . . Memorable Numbers . . . Konglish . . .
Shamanism . . . Top Buddhist Temples . . . Religion . . . Korean Culture
by the Book . . . Ginseng, Well-Being and Valentine's.

ARTS & ENTERTAINMENT **141**

City of Festivals . . . Traditional Korean Music and Dance . . . Richard
Choi's Top Nightspots . . . Western Classical Music . . . Leading Rock
Venues . . . Nanta . . . Mark Russell's Top Korean Films . . . K-Pop . . .
Big *Bang* . . . Art Museums . . . *Hallyu* . . . Top TV Dramas . . . Worlds
of Nam June Paik . . . *Manhwa* . . . Lotte World, Seoul Grand Park and
Seoul Land . . . Take Me Out to the Ball Game . . . Space Man . . .
Lucky Seven . . . The Sporting Life.

ECONOMY **177**

By the Numbers . . . Income . . . Top Korean Companies . . . Young-Iob
Chung's Five Aspects of the South Korean Economy . . . The Mighty
Jaebol . . . Motor Vehicles . . . IT . . . The Tycoon as Everyman . . .
North Korean Trade and GNP . . . Charge It . . . The Crisis of 1997 . . .
Seoul, A Bargain . . . The Face of Money.

THEN AND NOW **197**

Population Over Time . . . Ancient Gates and Walls . . . Top History
and Culture Museums . . . The American Empress . . . Transportation
Firsts . . . Colonial Times . . . The Korean War . . . The Rickshaw's
Rise and Fall . . . Andrei Lankov's Key Changes in Post-War Seoul . . .
Robert Neff's Ghost Stories . . . Skyscrapers . . . Haircuts . . . Fast Food
Firsts . . . Coffee.

POLITICS **219**

The National Scene . . . Branches of Government and Distribution of
Seats . . . Significant Post-War Leaders . . . The North-South Divide . . .
President Lee Myung-bak . . . National Assembly Building . . . Seoul
City Government . . . E-government.

CONTRIBUTING WRITERS **230**

Seoul:

A Timeline

6,000 years ago: Settlements along the Han River in what is now the city of Seoul.

57 BCE: Beginning of the Three Kingdoms period. Silla (57 BCE to 935 CE) in the southeastern part of the Korean Peninsula, Goguryeo (37 BCE to 668 CE) in the north, and Baekje (18 BCE to 660 CE) in the west form the building blocks of Korean civilization. Present-day Seoul lies roughly at the intersection of these kingdoms.

372: Buddhism introduced to Korea from China.

392-551: Battles amongst the kingdoms for control of the Han River Valley and Seoul. The Seoul area is, at different points, under the possession of all three kingdoms, and after 551 is under Silla rule.

618: Tang Dynasty comes to power in China and allies with Silla Kingdom in helping defeat Baekje and Goguryeo Kingdoms.

668-935: Unified Silla Period in which Baekje and Goguryeo are subsumed under the Silla Kingdom. Buddhism expands, many temples are built and the arts flourish. The Chinese, who wish to control the entire Korean Peninsula, are rebuffed by Silla whose domain is roughly that of the current Republic of Korea (South Korea) and Democratic People's Republic of Korea (North Korea).

918: Goryeo Kingdom is established with a capital at Gaeseong, about 60 kilometers (40 miles) north of Seoul. Buddhism continues to be dominant, but Confucianism is also a powerful force.

935: Goryeo Kingdom replaces Silla Kingdom.

1067: Seoul is designated one of three sub-capitals. It grows as a city and palaces are built.

1105: A palace is erected on the site of what would later become Cheongwadae, the official residence of the South Korean president.

1231: Mongols invade Korea, occupy Seoul, and remain a presence in Korea for a century and a half.

1392: Joseon Kingdom is founded by General Yi Seong-gye who overthrows the failing Goryeo Kingdom. Joseon lasts until 1910, and emphasizes Confucian precepts and practices.

1394: The capital of the Joseon Kingdom is established in Seoul. The city, traditionally known as Hanyang, is renamed Hanseong. In the following decade, Seoul's walls and gates are erected and Gyeongbokgung Palace is constructed.

1418: King Sejong the Great takes the throne; his 32-year reign results in numerous advances for Korea and its capital. Seoul's population tops 100,000.

The Joseon Kingdom (1392-1910)

Seoul's status as capital and leading city is directly linked to the rise of the Joseon Kingdom

Joseon, which means "land of the morning calm," was founded in 1392 when General Yi Seong-gye overthrew the failing Goryeo regime. Two years later, the capital of the new kingdom was moved to Hanyang (present day Seoul). Seoul's spectacular mountains and Han River location made it easy to defend and an ideal site for trade. It was also highly desirable from the standpoint of *pungsu-jiri* (natural earth-based forces believed to affect human fortunes).

The fledgling capital took shape rapidly. In the 1390s Gyeongbokgung Palace was constructed, and city walls and gates erected. City planning was completed by 1405, and Seoul's current lay-out reflects this early Joseon blueprint.

The Joseon Kingdom established Confucianism as the state religion. Core Confucian beliefs include filial piety (respect for elders and ancestors), social hierarchy and patriarchy.

During Joseon rule, high-level exam-based civil service positions became the entry into elite society. Education, at least for a certain strata of society, was much valued. Consequently, Seoul solidified its position as not just the political and administrative capital, but also Korea's knowledge center.

Joseon society was dominated by scholar-aristocrats; below them lay a professional class, and then common people such as merchants and tradesmen. Occupying the lowest rungs of society were servants and serfs.

During this era, Korea had relations with China, and was invaded by Japan and Manchuria, but was otherwise largely isolated, particularly from the West.

The Joseon Kingdom fell with Japan's late nineteenth century rise as Asia's dominant power. A final gasp was the 1897 declaration of King Gojong as Emperor of Korea; however, this attempt at asserting Korean sovereignty was short-lived, and a 1905 treaty gave Japan substantial power over Korea. In 1910 Japan occupied Korea and the Joseon Kingdom was finished. Nonetheless, Joseon's influence on the city of Seoul, and the country as a whole, still resonates to this day.

1592-98: Japanese invasions produce major damage, and Gyeongbokgung Palace, among other Seoul monuments, palaces, shrines and government buildings, is destroyed.

Bio King Sejong the Great (1397-1450)

Scholar, swordsman, musician, linguist and poet, Sejong the Great ranks as Korea's most respected king.

The third son of King Taejong, Sejong assumed power as a 21-year-old upon the abdication of his father in 1418. Sejong was the fourth king of Joseon and ruled for 32 years. During his reign, the Hall of Worthies was established. This fabled institute gathered together the leading intellects of the time to set down knowledge in diverse areas including agriculture, geography, statecraft, astronomy and medicine.

Sejong led troops in repelling Jurchen invaders from Manchuria, and in so doing established Korea's northern border at roughly the upper limit of present-day North Korea.

During Sejong's rule, a number of learned works were published, including a Korean encyclopedia of medicine. Sejong advocated the study of religion and the arts, yet also favored practical endeavors including taxonomy, cartography, and the establishment of archives. His Hall of Worthies developed rain gauges well ahead of the Europeans, as well as a system of moveable type that preceded Gutenberg.

Sejong was an avid proponent of Confucianism, a key element of the Joseon Kingdom. This is an important legacy, but his central role in developing the Korean alphabet, Hangeul, represents his greatest achievement. This simple yet sophisticated system is still in use today, and has proved vital in promoting literacy at all levels of Korean society.

Sejong was the rare king whose wisdom matched his power, and who was able to garner the respect of his subjects and make lasting contributions to the nation over which he ruled.

They said it

"He who risks death shall live, and he who seeks life shall die."
– Admiral Yi Sun-shin (1545-1598). Admiral Yi employed "turtle ships"
(*geobooksun*), spiked iron-clad vessels fitted with cannons, to
shrewdly and courageously defend Korea from attack in 1592.

1627, 1636: Manchurians invade from the north, again destroying much of Seoul (which had been rebuilt following previous invasions).

1790s: Catholicism establishes a foot-hold in Korea.

1867: Gyeongbokgung Palace is reconstructed.

1876: A forced treaty opens Korea up to trade with Japan, ending Korea's isolation.

1897: The Korean Empire is proclaimed to assert Korean sovereignty in light of Japan's increased military power, and to differentiate Korea from a weakening China.

1898: Construction completed on Seoul's Myeongdong Cathedral, whose French Gothic style would become the standard for Korean Catholic churches. Myeongdong Cathedral served as a safe house for political protests in the 1980s, notably the June 1987 pro-democracy rallies.

1904-05: Japan triumphs in its war with Russia; this victory, coupled with its 1895 defeat of China in the Sino-Japanese war, establishes Japan as the preeminent Asian power. A 1905 treaty between Japan and Korea renders Korea a protectorate of Japan.

1910: Japan annexes Korea and designates Seoul (which is renamed Keijo or Gyeongseong in Korean) the colonial capital. (See "Then and Now" chapter for details).

TAKE 5 CHOE KWANG-SHIK'S FIVE
TREASURES FROM THE NATIONAL
MUSEUM OF KOREA

Choe Kwang-shik, Ph.D., is the Director General of the National Museum of Korea. He previously served as a history professor at Korea University, as Director of the Korea University Museum and as head of the Society for Korean Ancient History.

The National Museum of Korea (NMK) was established in 1945 and is a sanctuary for over 5,000 years of Korean art and culture. Its mission is to make Korean culture accessible to a national and global audience, and it contains more than 200,000 cultural relics and artifacts.

The NMK relocated to Seoul's Yongsan area in 2005, and the new building ranks as the world's sixth largest museum in terms in floor space. The NMK's design represents a contemporary interpretation of traditional Korean architecture, and the grounds in Yongsan Family Park feature a pond, streams and landscaped gardens.

1. **Goguryeo Mural Paintings.** Mural paintings of the Goguryeo Kingdom (37 years BCE to 668 CE) portray a variety of types of people from 1,600 years ago, and vividly depict the daily lives, religion and thoughts of the Goguryeo people. These images also reveal the international relations and cultural interactions of a society during a time of territorial expansion and warfare.

2. **Gold Crown.** National Treasure No. 191 was excavated from the Hwangnam-daechong royal tomb in Gyeongju in southeastern Korea. The crown features upright ornaments as well as many gold spangles and pieces of comma-shaped jade hanging from its headband. The upright branch and antler type decorations symbolize the owner, a king or queen, who provided a connection between heaven and earth. Similar upright ornaments are found on the crowns of Siberian shamans, as well as on crowns excavated from Pazyryk tombs (circa 300 BCE) in the Altai mountains in southern Siberia, suggesting

cultural interactions with this region. This is an area where present day China, Mongolia and Kazakhstan converge, roughly 4,000 kilometers (2,500 miles) from Korea. This gold crown symbolizes supreme royal power and dignity, and represents the most advanced golden culture of the millennium kingdom of Silla (57 BCE to 935 CE).

3. **Pensive Bodhisattva.** National Treasure No. 83 dates from the seventh century, stands 91 cm (36 inches) tall and weighs 112 kg (247 pounds). The sculpture is made of gilt bronze and shows the Buddha in a meditation posture with one leg crossed and the other pendant, while one hand lightly touches the cheek. The image is simple, natural and gentle, with refined contours of the body and draperies. The Buddha's enigmatic smile is admired for its suggestion of the sublime.

4. **Goryeo Dynasty Incense Burner.** National Treasure No. 95 is made of celadon, a jade-colored ceramic highly characteristic of Korean pottery. It features a burner, a support and a cover to put out the incense. The piece features an openwork design and is an outstanding example of Goryeo-era (918 to 1392) celadon, a style that is loved internationally. Various techniques including incising, relief, and inlaying were used to create this functional object, a perfect and beautiful work of art.

5. **Ten-Story Pagoda.** National Treasure No. 86 stands 13.5 m (44 feet) tall and was originally erected at the Gyeongcheonsa temple site in 1348 during the Goryeo Dynasty. On its base are three tiers of delicate carvings of lions, *arhats* (Buddhists who have attained enlightenment) and scenes from a popular novel. In the central part of the towering pagoda, a number of groups of Buddhas and Bodhisattvas are represented inside architectural settings that feature minutely carved roofs, rafters and balustrades.

1919: On March 1 members of the Korean independence movement *Samil Undong* read a declaration in Seoul's Tapgol (Pagoda) Park, as well as at over 1,500 other locations around Korea.

1926: The Japanese administration completes construction on Seoul City Hall.

1938: The Samsung Group is founded. Samsung today is Korea's largest conglomerate and one of the world's biggest producers of computer chips, display panels, electronic goods, cell phones and ships.

1945: The occupation ends with Japan's surrender to the Allies. Korea is partitioned into North and South, with the U.S. occupying the southern sector and the Soviets the north. Seoul finally receives the name "Seoul."

1946: Seoul National University, Korea's most prestigious institution of higher learning, opens.

1948: The Republic of Korea (South Korea) is founded, as is the Democratic People's Republic of Korea (North Korea).

1950-53: Korean War. Massive destruction and many deaths in Seoul. Over one million people leave the city, although many return at war's end. (See "Then and Now" chapter for details).

1956: First television broadcast in Korea. Five years later, the television arm of the Korean Broadcast System debuts and provides the nation's first large-scale TV service.

1958: Gimpo in western Seoul becomes an international airport. Following the 2001 opening of Incheon International Airport, Gimpo is used chiefly for domestic flights.

1962: Namdaemun is designated Korea's first national treasure. Namdaemun, or South Gate, was completed in 1398 and survived both the Japanese occupation and the Korean War. Mapo, Seoul's first large scale high-rise apartment complex, is completed.

1966-70: Kim Hyeon-ok is elected mayor of Seoul and a period of rapid development and modernization begins. Streetcars are removed and new highways, overpasses, underpasses and tunnels are built. Cheonggyecheon Stream is paved over and an elevated highway built over it. Substandard housing is removed or renovated.

1967: Hyundai Motor Car Company founded. It now produces nearly four million vehicles annually, and South Korea is the world's fifth largest vehicle maker.

1968: Development begins on Yeouido, technically an island in the Han River. Yeouido contains apartment high-rises as well as the National Assembly building (opened in 1975), the 63 City building, the Korea Stock Exchange, and the headquarters of broadcasting studios, banks and insurance companies.

1968: A team of North Korean commandos reaches the foot of Mount Bugaksan behind the presidential residence, Cheongwadae ("the Blue House"), in an attempt to assassinate then President Park Chung-hee.

1969: Construction completed on the Hannam Bridge signaling the beginning of major development south of the Han River. The area is now a populous and powerful business, retail and residential district. Gyeongbu Expressway linking Seoul and Busan (South Korea's second-largest city) is completed the following year. Namsan Tower, now known as N Seoul Tower, is erected.

1970s: The South Korean economy exhibits spectacular growth and becomes known as "the Miracle on the Han River."

1970-1975: Seoul's population mushrooms, increasing by over 300,000 yearly and causing housing shortages. Rapid development continues, particularly south of the Han River.

1972: President Park Chung-hee establishes the Fourth Republic and bans political demonstrations and other acts of opposition to the government.

1973: 400,000 Christians gather in what is now Yeouido Park to listen to American preacher Billy Graham. In 1984 Pope John Paul II also attracts a major Yeouido audience.

1974: Seoul's first subway line begins operation. Line number nine debuted in 2009, and the system now records more than eight million passenger trips daily.

1978: Opening of the Sejong Center for the Performing Arts, the capital's leading venue for arts and culture.

1979: President Park Chung-hee is assassinated. KOEX (later renamed COEX) exhibition center opens. It later becomes a major complex featuring a convention center, hotels, mall and office tower.

1980: Anti-martial law and pro-democracy protests in May. In the southwestern city of Gwangju, the Gwangju Uprising is put down. N Seoul Tower on Namsan Mountain is opened to the public and becomes a major tourist attraction.

1981: Seoul is awarded the 1988 Summer Olympics. Sanbo Engineering develops the first Korean computer, and by decade's end Korea is a major computer exporter.

1984: Seoul Grand Park (now home to a zoo, amusement park and the National Museum of Contemporary Art) opens; one million people visit on the first day.

They said it

"South Korea had scant tradition of Olympic involvement, was of little standing in international sport, was not high on the world's consciousness of Asia and, most significant, was not recognized politically by any of the Communist states."
– *Encyclopedia of the Modern Olympic Movement* (Greenwood Press 2004) describing South Korea's seemingly unlikely successful bid for the 1988 Olympics. Seoul beat out Nagoya, Japan for the honor.

Late-1980s: Government initiates the "Two Million Home Construction Plan" and constructs five new satellite towns around Seoul to deal with congestion, lack of housing and soaring prices in the capital city. Continued subway construction spurs development and the creation of "sub-downtowns" further from the city center.

1986, 1987: Seoul hosts the 1986 Asian Games and nearly 5,000 athletes from 27 countries participate. Pro-democracy student protests and labor unrest occur in Seoul and other Korean cities.

1988: Seoul hosts the Summer Olympics and welcomes 8,400 athletes from 159 nations. Korea finishes fourth in the medal count. Seoul's population surpasses 10 million.

1989: Lotte World, the world's largest indoor theme park, opens in Jamsil.

1990s: The Republic of Korea solidifies its reputation as a democracy with fair elections, a free press, a full range of personal and political liberties and civilian control over the military.

1994: Seoul celebrates its six hundredth anniversary as Korea's capital. A time capsule containing 600 cultural properties on film and CD is buried in a specially designed square in Namsangol Hanok Village. The capsule is to be opened in 2394.

Mid-1990s: In recognition of its evolution as a city, plans are made to improve Seoul culturally, environmentally and recreationally.

The Olympics and World Cup

The 1988 Seoul Olympics represented the arrival of Seoul on the world stage, and the event was both cause and effect of South Korea's steady post-Korean War march toward modernity, prosperity and democracy.

The idea of hosting the Olympics was proposed in the late 1970s by then-President Park Chung-hee and pursued by his successor, Chun Doo-hwan.

The Seoul Olympics were the second ever held in Asia (Tokyo hosted in 1964) and were an enormous success. There had been widespread boycotts of the previous three Olympics (held in Montreal, Moscow and Los Angeles) and the world community was hungry for an Olympic success; Seoul delivered on all counts. The 1988 Games welcomed 159 nations and nearly 8,400 athletes. Only a handful of countries stayed home, North Korea amongst them.

The Games had a touching and dramatic opening when 76-year-old Sohn Kee-chung carried the torch into the Olympic Stadium. Sohn had been the first Korean ever awarded an Olympic medal when he won the marathon at the 1936 Games in Berlin. He had been forced, however, to compete as a member of the Japanese delegation because Korea was at that time under Japanese rule.

South Korea put on an excellent showing at the Games, finishing fourth in medals behind the USSR, East Germany and the U.S. The Korean delegation was particularly strong in archery, capturing a total of six medals. Other standout performers in Seoul included U.S. swimmer Matt Biondi and sprinter Florence Griffith Joyner.

The Olympic bid and the Games themselves, which came to fruition under President Roh Tae-woo's administration, brought global attention to South Korea. The event served as a catalyst for democratization as worldwide scrutiny made political compromise with reformers a necessity.

The 1988 Olympics remain a source of pride for Koreans, but there is also a very tangible legacy to the games. The Seoul subway system was expanded and other infrastructure upgraded. The

70,000-seat Olympic Stadium and Jamsil Sports Complex are still in use. The expansive Olympic Park, with its many walking trails and outdoor sculptures, remains a sanctuary for Seoulites in need of a respite from the pressures of city life.

Fourteen years after the Olympics, Seoul was the site of another big party – the 2002 World Cup. The tournament was organized jointly by South Korea and Japan, and over 27 million fans attended matches held at stadiums in ten cities in each country.

Seoul's World Cup Stadium hosted three games, including a semi-final match between Germany and South Korea. This game electrified the city, and the South Korean squad's dedicated fans became known as the "Red Devils." In downtown Seoul, City Hall Plaza became a sea of red as roughly two million fans donned red jerseys and packed the area to cheer on the South Korean side.

South Korea finished a strong fourth (behind Brazil, Germany and Turkey) in the 32-team tournament and received the award for most entertaining team. Star player and team captain Hong Myung-bo was named the third most outstanding player of the tournament.

Pride in South Korea's 2002 accomplishments on the soccer field endures, but so does Seoul World Cup Stadium, the 66,000-seat high-tech venue constructed for the event. Shaped like a traditional Korean kite, the stadium is still used by the FC Seoul Soccer team, and the stadium complex includes a mall, wedding hall and cinema. Visitors can relive memories of the 2002 semifinal match at the on-site World Cup Museum.

World Cup Stadium also forms part of a series of five connected parks in western Seoul that include a nine-hole golf course and other athletic facilities. The stadium and parks were constructed in an area that used to serve as Seoul's principal landfill, an example of turning trash into treasure.

1995: The Internet comes to Korea. The country goes on to become one of the world's most wired countries and develop a powerful IT industry. In 1999, Cyworld (Korea's largest online social networking site) is launched, beating MySpace and Facebook to the punch.

1996: South Korea becomes a member of the Organization for Economic Cooperation and Development (OECD), signaling its status as an advanced, industrialized economy. Korea is only the second Asian nation (after Japan) to be accorded membership.

1997: Kim Dae-jung is elected president and inaugurates the "Sunshine Policy" to develop more open relations with North Korea. In December, fall-out from the Asian financial crisis results in the government agreeing to IMF measures to stabilize South Korea's currency, the won. After decades of spectacular growth, the South Korean economy hits a speed bump.

2000: President Kim Dae-jung and North Korean leader Kim Jong-il meet in the North Korean capital of Pyeongyang. The summit represents the first meeting between heads of the two countries in 50 years. Kim becomes Korea's first Nobel laureate when he is awarded the Nobel Peace Prize.

2001: Incheon International Airport opens. In 2009 it is named the world's best airport by Skytrax, and ranks twelfth in international passenger volume.

Early 2000s: Korean popular culture wave crests and television dramas such as *Winter Sonata* became huge hits abroad. The wave spreads to music, film and other areas and Korea becomes a major entertainment exporter.

2002: Seoul serves as one of the host cities for the 2002 World Cup. The opening game of the tournament is played at World Cup Stadium and South Korea's boisterous fans earn the nickname the "Red Devils."

2003: The Hi-Seoul Festival debuts.

2004: President Roh Moo-hyun vows to move the capital from Seoul to South Chungcheong Province, 120 kilometers (75 miles) away. The move was expected to be fully executed by 2030, but the courts rule the move unconstitutional.

2005: A renovated Cheonggyecheon Stream reopens decades after being subsumed under concrete. Seoul Forest, located on the site of the former Ttukseom Sports Park, also opens, as does the new National Museum of Korea building.

2006: Korea's highest grossing movie at the box office, *The Host* (about a monster arising from the Han River), is released.

2007: Lee Myung-bak, a former Seoul mayor and CEO of Hyundai Engineering and Construction, is elected President of Korea. Ban Ki-moon, a former Minister of Foreign Affairs and Trade, is elected Secretary General of the United Nations.

2008: Namdaemun Gate, National Treasure No. 1, is damaged by an arsonist. Construction begins on a new Seoul City Hall which will have a "blue wave" look and feature environmentally friendly design elements. The new building will include a library, concert hall and look-out. Seoul hosts the World Design Olympiad.

2009: Former President Roh Moo-hyun commits suicide, and thousands pay their respects in a funeral in downtown Seoul. The 19,000-square-meter (4.7 acre) Gwanghwamun Square, on the site of what was the main thoroughfare during the Joseon Kingdom, opens. Former president and Nobel Prize winner Kim Dae-jung dies.

2010: Seoul serves as "World Design Capital" and hosts the G-20 Economic Summit.

Essentials

Seoul is the capital of the Republic of Korea. It is also the country's most populous and economically powerful city, and its educational and cultural center. It is divided administratively into 25 districts or "*gu*," and 522 neighborhoods or "*dong*." Seoul has served as capital since 1394.

Name: Seoul has gone by many names in its long history including Hanyang and Hanseong. It has been known as Seoul ("capital" in Korean) since 1945.

Location: Seoul is in the northwest part of South Korea, about 50 kilometers (30 miles) from the North Korean border. Seoul lies roughly halfway down (or up) the Korean Peninsula, 40 kilometers (25 miles) east of the West Sea (also known as the Yellow Sea) port city of Incheon. The Han River flows through Seoul from east to west in a wavy "w" pattern, and the city is surrounded by mountains.

Area: The city covers 605 square kilometers (234 square miles). By comparison, the five boroughs of New York City comprise 790 square kilometers (305 square miles), and Greater London, England is 1,580 square kilometers (610 square miles).

They said it

Latitude and longitude: Seoul is located at 37.34 N latitude and 126.59 E longitude. These coordinates put the city at roughly the same latitude as Tokyo, San Francisco, Washington, D.C., and Lisbon, and along a similar longitude as Pyeongyang, North Korea; Timor-Leste, East Timor; and Australia's Great Victoria Desert.

Distance from Seoul to:

Pyeongyang, North Korea: 195 km (121 miles); **Beijing, China:** 958 km (596 miles); **Tokyo, Japan:** 1,159 km (720 miles); **Manila, the Philippines:** 2,614 km (1,624 miles); **Mumbai, India:** 5,614 km (3,489 miles); **Moscow, Russia:** 6,615 km (4,111 miles); **Sydney, Australia:** 8,304 km (5,160 miles); **London, England:** 8,864 km (5,509 miles); **Los Angeles, USA:** 9,585 km (5,956 miles); **Toronto, Canada:** 10,607 km (6,592 miles); **Lagos, Nigeria** 12,415 km (7,715 miles); **Sao Paulo, Brazil:** 18,340 km (11,396 miles).

Did you know...

that Seoul ranked number three in a January 2010 *New York Times* article entitled "The 31 Places to Go in 2010"? Writes *The Times*: "Forget Tokyo. Design aficionados are now heading to Seoul." A diverse group of destinations rounded out the top five on *The Times*' list: Sri Lanka, Argentina's Patagonia wine country, Mysore (the south Indian city of palaces), and Copenhagen, Denmark.

Population: Seoul's population is 10.45 million people, distributed over 4.1 million households. The population is roughly divided between those living north and south of the Han River. Seoul occupies less than one percent of South Korea geographically, but contains over a fifth of the nation's population.

The number of people in the Seoul National Capital Area, which takes in Seoul City, Incheon City and Gyeonggi Province, is more than double the city number, placing metropolitan Seoul among the world's most populous urban areas. The capital region's population represents about half of South Korea's 48.5 million people. There are roughly 229,000 foreigners living in Seoul, a number equivalent to the population of Birmingham, Alabama; Saskatoon, Canada or Swansea, Wales.

Time zone: Korea Standard Time (KST). KST is nine hours ahead of Coordinated Universal Time (UTC) or Greenwich Mean Time (GMT). This is 14 hours ahead of North American Eastern Standard Time (when daylight savings is not in effect). South Korea does not use daylight savings time.

System of measurement: Metric.

Did you know. . .

that U.S. President Barack Obama is an aficionado of taekwondo, South Korea's national sport? Obama practiced taekwondo for several years while serving as a state senator in Illinois, and on his 2009 visit to Seoul was presented with an honorary black belt and taekwondo uniform by South Korean President Lee Myung-bak.

TAKE 5 **FIVE MOST POPULOUS**
SOUTH KOREAN CITIES

1. **Seoul** 10.5 million
2. **Busan** 3.5 million (on the southeastern coast, 327 km/203 mi. SE of Seoul)
3. **Incheon** 2.6 million (on the west coast, 40 km/25 mi. W of Seoul)
4. **Daegu** 2.5 million (inland in the southeast, 236 km/147 mi. SE of Seoul)
5. **Daejeon** 1.5 million (inland in west-central S. Korea, 150 km/93 mi. S of Seoul)

Area and country code: The country code for South Korea is 82 and the city code for Seoul is 02 (not used if calling locally). If calling from outside Korea, drop the "0" in "02." Mobile phone numbers do not include the Seoul city code; the country code (82) is followed by the prefix 10, 11, 16, 17, 18, or 19, after which comes the phone number. Cell phones are available for rent at Incheon Airport and other locations.

Seoul city symbol: Haechi. Also known as *Haetae*, Haechi was chosen as city symbol in 2008. Haechi has a lion-like head and dog-like torso, and is a mythological figure known as a protector. Haechi's traditional self is represented in the statue in Gwanghwamun Gate, and in print he appears as a simple blue and white line drawing. Haechi's

Did you know. . .

that the Rose of Sharon is the Korean national flower? The *Mugunghwa*, which is indigenous to Korea, has been treasured for centuries, and Mugunghwa Country was a name given to the Silla Kingdom. The Rose of Sharon, which blooms from early July to October, is a hardy plant and Korea is home to more than 100 cultivated varieties.

Did you know. . .

that Seoul has 22 sister cities worldwide? Seoul's first sister, Taipei, Taiwan, arrived in 1968.

more fanciful self is a yellow mascot who has white mitten hands, a big smile and a prominent orange nose. The latter Haechi dispenses tips on life in Seoul to visitors and locals. Other prominent Seoul symbols and icons include the tiger, the pine tree and the gingko tree.

Slogans: "Soul of Asia" and "Hi Seoul." These mottos are used to denote Seoul's position as a leading Asian hub for business and tourist travel, as well as its status as a historic, culturally rich and open city.

ON AN AVERAGE DAY IN SEOUL . . .
- 254 babies are born
- 104 people die
- 203 couples get married
- 67 couples divorce
- 7,845 people move in or out of the city
- 19 construction permits are issued

They said it

"The heart of every Korean is in Seoul. Officials have town houses in the capital, and trust their businesses to subordinates for much of the year. Landed proprietors draw their rents and 'squeeze' the people on their estates, but are essentially living in the capital. Every man who can pay for food and lodging on the road trudges to the capital once or twice a year, and people who live in it, of whatever degree, can hardly be bribed to leave it, even for a few weeks. To the Korean it is the place in which alone life is worth living."

– British travel writer Isabella Lucy Bird from her 1898 book *Korea and her Neighbours*. Bird visited Korea four times during the mid-1890s.

SOUTH KOREAN DEMOGRAPHICS

Population: 48.5 million (25th largest of 237 worldwide)
Median age: 37.3
Population growth: .266 percent (178th of 223 worldwide)
Birth rate: 8.93 births/1,000 population (212th of 223 worldwide)

TAKE5 SAM HAMMINGTON'S TOP FIVE
THINGS YOU *MUST* BRING TO KOREA

Sam Hammington was born in 1979 and is a native of Australia. He is passionate about Korea and his adopted city of Seoul. He loves its peculiarities and idiosyncrasies, and all the things that make it unique. He is Korea's first foreign comedian, and can be seen on the long running local TV comedy program *Gag Concert*. He also co-hosts the popular radio show *Drive Time*, which is broadcast on 103.1 TBS eFM in Seoul.

1. Underwear.
I don't know about you, but my Mum always told me to never leave the house without a clean pair of underwear on. And as such, this ranks number one on my essentials list! It's a good thing I always listen to her, because Korean underwear just doesn't seem to fit right.

2. An iron liver.
The best way to develop a close relationship with anyone in Korea is through the art of drinking. And Koreans do like a good drink! Even if you are not a drinker, you will be expected to drink your share of beer and *soju* over a Korean barbeque dinner. Most social outings, and a good many business meetings, are held over a drink or three.

3. An open mind.
Korean culture has a structured hierarchy; as such, age is an important factor. Thus, when someone asks you how old you are, don't take

Urbanization: 81 percent
Life expectancy: 78.7 years. (Men: 75.5 years; women: 82.2 years). The combined figure is 40th of 224 worldwide.
Literacy (percentage over the age of 15 who can read and write): 97.9 percent.

offense. It's a way for the person to figure out how formal you will need to be with each other. Other questions that may put you on the back foot include "Are you married?" and "Do you have a boyfriend/ girlfriend?" Don't stress it, they're just icebreakers here in Korea.

4. An appetite for destruction.
There are plenty of exciting things to chow down on while in Korea. One of my personal favorites is the live baby octopus, a whole baby octopus wrapped around a chopstick. You've got to put it in your mouth quickly, then chew, chew, chew, before it sticks itself to the roof of your mouth, or finds its way into your nasal cavity. Some other good items are live prawns, ice-cold spicy noodles and plenty of hot, hot food!

5. A tie between a spork and deodorant.
Two things that you might have trouble finding in Korea are forks and deodorant. For those of you that have trouble using chopsticks, you should bring your own spork! In my opinion, it's a greatly underappreciated utensil in its combination of a spoon and fork. Also, Koreans don't seem to have the same underarm odor problems that many in the West do. Deodorant is something that you will struggle to find here, but believe me you are going to need it, especially if you come in the summer.

You Know You're From Seoul When . . .

- You think that South Korea's second largest city, Busan (population 3.5 million), is a quaint seaside town.
- If in need of a quiet place to clear your head, you visit the grounds of a 600-year-old palace.
- You think of cell phones as disposable, and replace yours every few months.
- You take it for granted that you can travel anywhere in the city, including the subway, day or night, without fear for your personal safety.
- You think a proper school day ends at 10 p.m. (Local students often attend after-school academies; sessions for teenagers can stretch into the night).
- Everyone seems to be related (you call people "older brother," "older sister," "aunt" and "uncle" instead of using their given names).
- You watch more TV on your phone while commuting than you do at home.
- You think a hike up Namsan Mountain (in the middle of Seoul) counts as a trip to the countryside.
- You're not sure if you believe that rain landing on your head causes baldness, but you're not taking any chances.
- You associate the smell of rotting gingko nuts with the start of autumn, but know that the spectacular colors to follow are more than worth it.
- You're blessed with the ability to simultaneously talk on the phone, watch TV, smoke a cigarette and drive.
- You wake up well before dawn to get on the road for your holiday getaway, thus avoiding the seven a.m. weekend-exodus rush hour.
- Fashion trends like mini-skirts or shawls hit like typhoons, and women wearing the item *du jour* are suddenly everywhere.
- You consider a 1.5-hour commute to work from a satellite suburb normal.
- You decide which restaurant or cafe to patronize based on the discounts you can get from your cell phone plan or credit card.
- You've been playing the videogame Starcraft at a PC *bang* (room) with your friends for over a decade.
- You order pickles with Italian food, and must have kimchi to accompany your meal, whether the cuisine is Indian, Mexican or North American.
- You accept the fact that when you visit a city park, the grassy portion is "off-limits," and is for admiring from the paved walkways.

Voting age: 19.

Military service: Mandatory for roughly two years, depending on the branch of service, for men aged 20 to 30. There are approximately 560,000 Republic of Korea soldiers on active duty.

TAKE5 FIVE ICONIC SEOUL LANDMARKS

1. **N Seoul Tower**. Constructed on Namsan Mountain in 1969 to transmit radio and television signals, N Seoul Tower is visible from many places in the city. Renovated in 2005, N Seoul Tower features a high-tech observatory, a café, a Korean style family eatery and a revolving restaurant.

2. **Gyeongbokgung Palace**. The expansive palace, completed in 1395, lies near Mount Bukhansan and was the principal home of the Royal Family during the Joseon Kingdom. It was burned down in the 1590s and rebuilt in 1868.

3. **Namdaemun Gate**. Built in 1398, National Treasure No. 1 stands at one of the city's busiest intersections, and perfectly captures the juxtaposition of feudal Seoul with the city's high-tech contemporary face. Namdaemun, also known as Great South Gate, is built of wood and stone with a tiled roof. It was badly damaged by a 2008 fire; renovations are expected to be completed by the end of 2012.

4. **Olympic Stadium**. The 70,000-seat Olympic Stadium is part of the Jamsil Sports Complex constructed for the 1988 Olympics. The stadium's curved design is inspired by a Joseon-era vase.

5. **Skyscrapers**. The 63 City building on Yeouido (60 above-ground floors), the Samsung Tower Palace luxury apartment complex (73 floors), and the Trade Tower (55 floors) are just a few of Seoul's many high-rises, a feature which has come to dominate the city in the last 25 years.

Driving: Vehicles drive on the right-hand-side. There are about three million cars registered in the city of Seoul, and over seven million in the metro area. Roads are usually in good repair, and signs for major arteries are in Korean and English. Local streets, however, are often not marked, and traffic in Seoul can be fierce. Most visitors find nego- tiating Seoul via its efficient public transportation system and plentiful private taxis a far better option than driving.

Languages (other than Korean): English is widely found on signs. Japanese and Chinese language signs are also found in some areas. Many Koreans speak at least some English, and most read it at a basic level or higher.

Currency: The Korean won. Exchange rates are always fluctuating, but very broadly speaking, the 1,000 won note has similar status as a U.S. one-dollar bill, and the 10,000 won note is similar to a U.S. ten- dollar bill or five-Euro note.

MAJOR HOLIDAYS
- **New Year's Day (January 1)**.
- **Seollal (Lunar New Year):** occurs in January or February. Most things are closed for three days, and many Koreans visit their home- towns and eat traditional foods.

Did you know. . .

that Koreans are much more likely to "Naver" (www.naver.com) something than Google it? Naver is far and away Korea's lead- ing search engine, and has a separate gaming portal that caters to Korea's avid on-line gaming community. Naver leads the pack chiefly because it provides a large amount of Korean language content. Another Korean language search engine, Daum (www. daum.net) is second to Naver. Google and Yahoo's Korean sites are not widely used.

- **Independence Movement Day (March 1)**: commemorates resistance to Japan's former occupation of Korea.
- **Labor Day (May 1)**.
- **Buddha's Birthday:** occurs in May according to the lunar calendar.
- **Children's Day (May 5)**: honors and supports children. Family outings to parks and zoos are common.
- **Memorial Day (June 6)**: National Cemetery in Seoul is the scene of a major ceremony honoring the nation's war dead.
- **Liberation Day (August 15)**: commemorates the liberation of Korea from Japanese rule in 1945.
- **Chuseok or Harvest Moon Festival**: takes place in September or October depending on the lunar calendar. Koreans often journey home to be with family and celebrate the fall harvest.
- **National Foundation Day (October 3)**: honors the founding of the Korean nation in 2333 BCE.
- **Christmas Day (December 25)**.

Other special days: Parents' Day (May 8), Constitution Day (July 17), Hangeul (Korean alphabet) Day (October 9).

ROYAL PALACES
Seoul's palaces date to the Joseon Kingdom (1392-1910), and are an essential aspect of the city. The suffix "*gung*" means "palace" in Korean.

Did you know. . .

that 61 percent of Korean high school graduates enter college? In Japan the figure is 46 percent, in Great Britain 55 percent and in Germany 34 percent.

Gyeongbokgung. The Kingdom's chief palace was built in 1395 shortly after Seoul was designated capital. The palace's location was established according to principles of *pungsu-jiri*, (the energy emanating from the earth and the elements). Mount Bugaksan lies behind Gyeongbokgung, and Gwanghwamun Gate serves as its entrance. Sejongno, the busy artery leading to the palace, was once the Kingdom's main thoroughfare, and is now home to Gwanghwamun Square (as well as a number of important contemporary buildings).

Gyeongbokgung, like most everywhere in Seoul, has paid a heavy

World Design Capital

Seoul is recognized as a world center for industrial and urban design, and was named World Design Capital for 2010 by the International Council of Societies of Industrial Design. The designation takes in the calendar years of 2009 and 2010, and includes competitions, exhibitions, forums, and festivals highlighting Seoul's innovative design scene. For more information, visit http://wdc2010.seoul.go.kr/eng/index.jsp.

The Dongdaemun Design Plaza (DDP), designed by acclaimed British-Iraqi architect Zaha M. Hadid, is the city's signature building in its role as Design Capital. The DDP and accompanying park incorporate an ancient city wall in their design, and are next to the Dongdaemun Market, a world center for fashion design, production and sales. The plaza will support the fashion industry, while the park will provide added green space in central Seoul, and highlight the area's culture and history. The DDP complex will be completed in 2011.

Donggaemun Design Plaza is just one in a series of projects that have transformed, and are transforming, the face of Seoul. In this century alone, Incheon International Airport (2001), Seoul Plaza (2004), the National Museum of Korea building (2005), Cheonggyecheon Stream (2005), Seoul Forest (2005), price at the hands of occupiers and invaders. It was destroyed in the 1590s by the Japanese, and then abandoned for over 250 years before being rebuilt in 1868. During the Japanese occupation in the first part of the twentieth century, Gyeongbokgung was altered and large parts of it demolished. Much of Gyeongbokgung and its expansive grounds have now been restored and reconstituted. There are many elegant buildings to explore, lovely views throughout, and free guided tours. The National Folk Museum of Korea (which contains over 4,000 artifacts used by Koreans in their everyday lives in years past) and the National Palace Museum are also located on the palace grounds.

Gwanghwamun Square (2009) and the presidential museum Cheong Wa Dae Sarangchae (2010), are just some of the major projects that have been completed. Coming soon is a new City Hall building (2011), a renovated Seoul Station (2011), and, further on the horizon, a major upgrade to Seoul Grand Park and the creation of the Yongsan International Business District by Studio Daniel Libeskind. The "Yongsan Dream Hub," which will remake the area and cost more than $22.6 billion, is scheduled to be completed in 2016 and will include the world's second tallest building.

In addition to Hadid and Libeskind, a number of other global superstar architects, including Rem Koolhaas, Mario Botta, Jean Nouvel and Rafael Vinoly have designed commercial and institutional buildings in Seoul. In many cases, foreign architects work in conjunction with local firms, and South Korean architects have been behind a number of visionary projects constructed in the capital area in the last decade. Unlike some cities which are, in a sense, "finished," Seoul is still evolving; the various recent ventures are reinterpreting and renovating the city's past, and charting new directions for a capital that is both ancient and futuristic.

TAKE 5 **LARS VARGO'S TOP FIVE**
KOREAN READS

Lars Vargo is the founder and President of the Seoul Literary Society. He has a doctorate in Japanese history from the University of Stockholm, and is the author of many books. He has served as the Swedish Ambassador to South Korea since January 2006, and is keenly interested in literature, particularly as a means of understanding a nation and its people.

1. *The Dawn of Modern Korea - The Transformation in Life and Cityscape* **by Andrei Lankov (1963-).** Andrei Lankov was born and raised in Russia, but is a longtime Korea specialist who is an Associate Professor at Kookmin University in Seoul. He writes in English, Korean and Russian on North and South Korean history, politics and society. Lankov is well known for his realistic, critical and cynical views on North Korean society, but in *The Dawn of Modern Korea* he examines the history and society of South Korea in the twentieth century with curious eyes. He tells stories and anecdotes in a refreshing way, revealing interesting and unknown details about the everyday lives of Koreans in a period of great change.

2. *Ten Thousand Lives* **by Ko Un (1933-).** Translated by Brother Anthony of Taizé, Young-moo Kim and Gary Gach. Green Integer, 2005, 366 pages.

The poet Ko Un is believed to have been on the short list for the Nobel Prize in literature for many years. His *Ten Thousand Lives* is part of a project to document in the form of poems all the (interesting) people he has met in his life. Ko has produced approximately 140 volumes of poetry, fiction and essays in his lengthy career, and has received numerous awards both in Korea and abroad for his work. Ko is a former Buddhist monk whose poetry took on a nihilist bent in the 1960s. In the 1970s, he became a major figure in the democracy movement, and he was three times imprisoned for his outspoken views on free speech and human rights. He has written in many styles, and his "zen poetry" is filled with both insight and refreshing naïveté.

3. *The Book of Korean Shijo.* **Translated and edited by Kevin O'Rourke (1939-).** Harvard University Press, 2002, 219 pages. O'Rourke is an Irishman who came to Korea in 1964 as a young priest. He later received a doctorate in Korean literature from Yonsei University, and is a Professor Emeritus of Korean language and literature at Kyung Hee University in Seoul. In this volume he has collected classical Korean poems of the *sijo* form. Although not as compact as Japanese haiku, *sijo* are short poems following set patterns. A real treasure.

4. *The Coldest Winter - America and the Korean War* **by David Halberstam (1934-2007).** Hyperion, 2007, 719 pages. The Pulitzer Prize-winning American journalist's last, and perhaps best, book is a detailed description of the Korean War. The author sympathizes with the soldiers in the field while criticizing many of the commanders for taking wrong, and sometimes cowardly, decisions. The many pages disappear quickly, and the reader ends up with a feeling of having been part of the war.

5. *Korea at the Crossroads - The History and Future of East Asia* **by Bae Kichan (1962-).** Translated by Kim Jin. Happyreading, 2007, 488 pages. A refreshing and new analysis of Korean and East Asian history. The author believes that clashes between maritime and continental powers have been key in shaping the region over a period of centuries. The book gives a good overview of how Korean society has been formed, and is useful as reference material. Simply fascinating.

Bonus anthologies: *Modern Korean Fiction* **Edited by Bruce Fulton & Youngmin Kwon.** Columbia University Press, 2005, 416 pages. A good selection of stories by 22 representative Korean writers, including some North Korean authors. *Azalea - Journal of Korean Literature & Culture*, Korea Institute, Harvard University. An annually published anthology of fiction and poetry that began in 2007.

Deoksugung. Located in downtown Seoul near City Hall, Deoksugung was the last of the palaces to serve as a royal residence. Emperor Gojong lived at Deoksugung from 1897 to 1919, although he abdicated the throne in 1907. The compound is a mix of old, new, traditional Korean and Western structures. Deoksugung is in the heart of the action, and passers-by and office workers often relax on the grounds during their lunch break. There is a spectacular 30-minute changing of the guard ceremony held three times daily, and the palace grounds are home to Deoksugung Art Museum.

Gyeonghuigung. Gyeonghuigung was sometimes known as "West Palace" as it was in the city's western area during Joseon times. A number of historical dramas have been filmed at Gyeonghuigung, the filmmakers taking advantage of the palace's traditional sloping tiled roofs, which harmonize with the surrounding mountains. Gyeonghuigung features twice-weekly taekwondo performances and there are several attractions in the immediate vicinity, including the Seoul Museum of History and the Seoul Museum of Art.

Did you know. . .

that at Seoul post offices, in addition to mailing a letter, you can access the Internet for free, and even check your blood pressure?

TAKE**5** FIVE UNIQUE SEOUL
MEETING VENUES

There are many special places in Seoul available for meetings and receptions, as well as recreation and sightseeing. Seoul offers venues exhibiting great natural and architectural beauty, not to mention ones rich in culture and history. There are also trendy spots with a lively big city vibe. The Seoul Convention Bureau (www.miceseoul.com) has all the details.

1. **Fradia**. Elegant Fradia comes alive at night for fine Italian dining, concerts, meetings and receptions. The waterfront location on the Han's south side provides exceptional city and river views. www.fradia.co.kr.

2. **Aston House and the Jade Garden**. On the slopes of Achasan Mountain in northeast Seoul, these venues provide mountain and river views. Located in the same complex as the super deluxe W Seoul Walkerhill Hotel and the Sheraton Grande Walkerhill, the exclusive Aston House is a sanctuary just outside the hustle and bustle of the central city. The Jade Garden, a separate facility, is a larger outdoor space nearby. www.sheratonwalkerhill.co.kr.

3. **Samcheonggak**. Located in the forested hills of northern Seoul, Samcheonggak is an enchanting spot. It was founded in 1972 as a venue for meetings between high-ranking government officials and is now a traditional culture and arts complex with a performance stage, Korean restaurant, wine bar and cultural experience hall. The traditionally designed building is popular for banquets, seminars and workshops, and the rustic setting is exquisite. www.samcheonggak.or.kr/.

4. **Yeong Bin Gwan**. Once known as the State Guest House, Yeong Bin Gwan was built in 1967 by the Korean government to welcome foreign visitors. It is now part of the Shilla Hotel, and is a spectacular setting for banquets and garden parties. The traditional two-story building reproduces the splendor of the Silla Kingdom, and is an elegant space with lovely views. www.shilla.net/en/seoul.

5. **Korea House**. Centrally located Korea House, operated by the Korea Cultural Heritage Foundation, is a wonderful place for groups to sample royal cuisine and enjoy cultural offerings, including traditional Korean performances and ceremonies. www.kangkoku.or.kr/eng.

Changgyeonggung and Jongmyo Royal Shrine. Changgyeonggung was constructed in 1483, and like all of Seoul's palaces, heavily damaged during 1590s invasions. It also suffered destruction from fires in 1624 and 1830. Changgyeonggung is linked by a footbridge to the Jongmyo Royal Shrine, and on its other side is connected to Changdeokgung Palace. Jongmyo Royal Shrine, a UNESCO World Heritage Site, was built in 1394 when the Joseon capital was established in Seoul. The shrine houses spirit tablets pertaining to Joseon royalty and other meritorious subjects. Ritual ceremonies, whose origins date to the fifteenth century, still take place in the shrine.

Changdeokgung Palace and its Secret Garden. Changdeokgung was built in 1405 and served as principal palace for approximately 300 years, a longer period than any of the other palaces. King Sejong, Korea's most famous ruler, spoke of it as an "ideal place." Behind Changdeokgung is another UNESCO World Heritage Site: Huwon, also known as the Secret Garden. The *ongnyucheon*, or stream, as well as the waterfall, pond, plants, trees, and palace pavilions form a harmonious, peaceful and elegant tableau. Joseon royalty would convene in this idyllic setting to study, write poetry and drink wine.

A COMPLETE CONVENTION CITY

Seoul is ranked in the top ten convention cities worldwide by both the International Congress and Convention Association and the Union of International Associations. The city hosts hundreds of international meetings every year, and more than 60 facilities are registered for hosting conventions (including 14 with a capacity of 1,000 people or more).

Seoul has 34 large-scale convention hotels, all of them in the super deluxe and deluxe category, as well as numerous government approved high-quality mid and budget-priced accommodations, designated as "Innostels." Seoul also features elegant traditional Korean guest houses, serviced residences (ideal for extended visits), and novel experiences including "temple stays" that are perfect for independent, leisure travelers.

In 2008, Seoul hosted the 22nd World Congress of Philosophy and the 18th World Congress on Safety and Health at Work, while 2009 brought the 35,000 delegate Herbalife Asia Pacific Extravaganza to the city. Major events in 2010 and beyond include SIGGRAPH Asia 2010 (20,000 participants), the 22nd World Congress of Dermatology (15,000 participants) and the 2016 Rotary International Annual Convention (50,000 participants).

Seoul continues to grow as a convention destination, and there are several new facilities scheduled to open in the next several years including Dongdaemun Design Plaza, the Seoul International

TAKE5 FIVE SEOUL CONVENIENCES

1. **Waiter Call Buttons.** In most restaurants and bars, you don't have to wait for your server if you require another drink, more napkins or extra sauce. There are little buttons on the table that you can push notifying your waiter or waitress that you are in need.

2. **Professional Designated Drivers.** This service is invaluable if you've had too much to drink and need to get yourself, and your car, home safely. In Korea, you can call a service that will come and drive you and your vehicle home for about $20.

3. **24-Hour Food Delivery.** You can get a bite to eat any time of day or night in Seoul, and you don't even need to step outside. A surprising range of restaurants deliver, including fast food chains like McDonald's.

4. **Convenience Stores.** These are located most everywhere and many are open 24-hours. They have everything from food, beer, stationery products, dog food and cigarettes to socks and aspirin. Most have areas inside or out where you can sit, eat, and drink.

5. **DMB, 3G, WiBro, and full bars (cell phone signal bars).** You can always connect to the phone and Internet in Seoul, no matter what your location, including underground in the subway, or on top of a mountain.

Financial Center and the Seoul International Exchange Center.

Choice can be overwhelming, but there are people in Seoul to help. The Seoul Convention and Visitors Bureau (www.miceseoul.com) serves as a one-stop resource for planning meetings and events in Seoul.

TOP CONVENTION CENTERS:
- **COEX World Trade Center.** A world-class exhibition destination, COEX spreads out over 225,000 square meters (2.4 million square

TAKE5 FIVE THINGS TO DO WITH
YOUR MOBILE PHONE IN SEOUL

1. **Watch television.** Since 2005, Korean cell phones have been able to receive digital television signals. Mass transit commuters often take advantage of this feature to catch up on the latest television dramas or sports highlights.

2. **Pay transit fares and buy snacks.** A chip in the phone can be charged with "T-money" that can be used to get on the subway or to make purchases at kiosks, convenience stores and vending machines. Parents can put T-money on a child's phone instead of handing over cash. Some taxis also take payment by mobile phone.

3. **Send someone a gift.** A person can purchase a gift from a merchant and it will show up on the recipient's phone as an icon—such as a pizza or tube of lipstick—which can then be redeemed.

4. **Turn on the heat, air conditioning or lights.** Seoul's newest luxury apartments like the Samsung Tower Palace allow residents to use their phone to remotely turn on the heat, AC or lights. No more coming home to a cold, dark apartment in winter (or a steamy one in summer). A phone can also be used to start a load of laundry, as well as monitor doors, windows and locks for security purposes.

5. **Banking.** An ATM or computer is not needed to check bank balances, transfer funds or send money; these tasks can all be accomplished from a mobile phone.

feet) on eight floors, and includes 36,000 square meters (387,500 square feet) of exhibition space. COEX features outstanding lodging, dining and shopping facilities, and is located in Samseong-dong in the heart of bustling Gangnam-gu. The World Trade Center Seoul and ASEM Tower are nearby. www.coex.co.kr/eng.

- **SETEC.** The Seoul Trade, Exhibition and Convention Center opened in 1999 and is operated by the Seoul Business Agency. It has three exhibition halls with 11,000 square meters (118,403 square feet) of floor space on a site of almost 32,000 square meters (344,445 square feet). www.setec.or.kr/eng.

- **aT Center.** The Agro Trade & Exhibition Center opened in 2002 and offers a full range of meeting, exhibition and convention facilities. It often hosts international fairs and exhibitions in the area of agriculture and food products and services. The aT Center is located in Yangjae-dong, in the thriving and upscale Seocho-gu south of the Han River. www.atcenter.co.kr/at_ahe.

- **Seoul Women's Plaza.** Opened in 2004 and specializing in events and programs geared toward women, Seoul Women's Plaza operates under the auspices of the Seoul Foundation of Women & Family. www.seoulwomen.or.kr/nhpeng.

MEDICAL TOURISM

Seoul is home to 56 major hospitals, as well as over 500 cosmetic surgery clinics and 11 comprehensive international clinics. South Korea has an impressive medical system, and boasts one of the world's leading treatment rates for stomach, liver and cervical cancer.

Increasing numbers of foreigners are coming to Korea for medical

Did you know...

that there are 95 embassies in Seoul? The capital is also home to numerous consulates, trade offices and agencies representing foreign countries and regions.

and health purposes – over 27,000 in 2008 and approximately 50,000 in 2009. The number of such visitors should hit 200,000 in 2013, and Korea's Health Industry Development Institute is devoted to promoting Korea as a premier destination for medical procedures. In 2010 Seoul played host to the Global Healthcare & Medical Tourism Conference, which brought attendees from over 25 countries to the city. People come to Korea for everything from dental care to cancer treatment to cosmetic surgery, and can obtain special medical tourist visas lasting from three months to a year.

Cosmetic surgery is common in Seoul, and the Apgujeong-dong area of Gangnam-gu is akin to Beverly Hills, with plentiful plastic surgery clinics, great shopping and lots of trendy places to eat and drink.

Seoul's Medical Tourism Center (www.seoulmedicaltour.com) is a one-stop clearing house for information on a range of medical procedures available in the capital city. It provides information on Korean medical institutions that treat foreigners, as well as details on visas and tours. The office is located in downtown Seoul and can be reached at 82-2-2268-1339 (don't use the 82 or 2 if dialing from Seoul). Visitors can use body composition and skin analyzers, as well as stress and blood pressure monitors free of charge. Medical tourism information is also offered at Incheon Airport, which has a Medical Tourism Information Center and lounge specifically for medical tourists. Information on

Did you know. . .

that South Koreans, and Seoulites, are among the planet's most wired people? Korea has 37.5 million Internet users (tenth in the world), 45.6 million mobile phones and 21.3 million land lines. Mobile phone use is 93 percent, and each Korean household has, on average, 2.73 cell phones. The Internet penetration rate is the highest of any OECD nation, and Korea is number two in the world in broadband access (after the Netherlands).

medical tourism can also be found online through www.visitkorea. or.kr (from the "Sights, Activities & Events" tab, click on "Themed Travel" and "Medical Tourism"). This site links to a searchable database of medical institutions and procedures, and is reachable by phone at 82-2-1330 (don't use the 82 or 2 if dialing from Seoul). Another source of information is Medical Korea (www.medicalkorea.or.kr).

TAKE5 FIVE THINGS NAMED AFTER KING SEJONG (1397-1450), KOREA'S MOST FAMOUS RULER

King Sejong's rule was marked by an explosion of achievements in the arts and sciences. It was during his reign that Hangeul, the Korean phonetic alphabet, was developed.

1. **Sejong Cultural Center.** Opened in 1978, the Sejong Center is located on Sejongno Boulevard. This was at one time the Joseon Kingdom's main thoroughfare, and was known as the "Street of Six Ministries." The Sejong Center represents the heart of Korean culture and includes the 3,000 seat Grand Theater.

2. **Sejong Hotel.** A deluxe 273-room hotel that opened in 1966 in the Myeong-dong area.

3. **Sejong University.** Founded in 1940, Sejong University was formerly Soodo Women's College of Education. It first admitted male students in 1978, and has been known as Sejong University since 1987. It is located near the Children's Grand Park subway station.

4. **Sejong Institute.** Founded in 1983, the Sejong Institute is a private think tank performing research and analyses in the areas of foreign affairs, security and national unification.

5. **Sejong City.** A proposed administrative center south of Seoul near the city of Daejeon. It was planned as the future home for much of the South Korean national government, but court rulings and political resistance have left its future up in the air and it remains a work in progress.

The DMZ

The DMZ (Demilitarized Zone) is an enduring reminder of the Cold War and the ongoing tensions between North and South Korea. The DMZ is a 4 kilometer (2.5 mile) wide band that stretches the length of the Korean Peninsula, and divides a people who share a common language, history and ethnicity into two very separate Koreas. Technically, the two countries are still at war, and the DMZ is part of the 1953 armistice agreement.

Visitors to the DMZ include history and military buffs, as well as those keen to get close to North Korea (truly a Hermit Kingdom). Another group that has found the area fertile ground, literally, are naturalists and wildlife biologists. There is no development within the DMZ, and this has made it a de facto sanctuary for flora and fauna whose habitats have elsewhere been damaged or destroyed.

The DMZ lies a mere 55 kilometers (28 miles) from Seoul, but the area is heavily guarded and you can't just pop in unannounced. If you wish to visit, you must travel as a member of a tour. Itineraries vary, but typically include the Bridge of Freedom, Dora Observatory (from which North Korea is quite visible) and Panmunjeom, the Joint Security Area (JSA) where negotiations took place to end the fighting in the Korean War. During the warmer months, an unexpected delight is the journey down into the deliciously cool Third Tunnel of Aggression.

The tunnel was discovered in 1978 and is one of several dug by the North Koreans, presumably to infiltrate and attack the South Korean side. The weight of history bears down upon the DMZ installations, as is the knowledge that the forbidden, the unknown, the menacing—North Korea—lies a stone's throw away.

Tens of thousands have visited the DMZ, but Lotte World it's not — a passport is required, and there is a dress code (business casual is fine). The tours, which need to be reserved in advance, are conducted by U.S. Army and Republic of Korea soldiers. A number of companies offer tours; excursions generally leave from Seoul in the morning and return in the mid or late afternoon.

They said it

"1. A military demarcation line shall be fixed and both sides shall withdraw two (2) kilometers from this line so as to establish a demilitarized zone between the opposing forces. A demilitarized zone shall be established as a buffer zone to prevent the occurrence of incidents which might lead to a resumption of hostilities. 7. No person, military or civilian, shall be permitted to cross the military demarcation line unless specifically authorized to do so by the Military Armistice Commission."

– Article 1, points number 1 and 7 from the July 27, 1953 Korean War Armistice Agreement.

GETTING AROUND

First the good news: Seoul is very safe, and almost all destinations are easily accessed by taxi, subway, or bus. Cabs are reasonable and the subway is wonderfully efficient and user-friendly.

On the downside, unless you are going to a landmark like a big hotel, the 63 City building, or Gyeongbokgung Palace, finding your way can sometimes be challenging. Many streets are not marked, and building numbers are rarely in sequential order. Taxi drivers know the major spots, and it helps if you write your destination on a piece of

Did you know...

that Seoul-based *Chosun Ilbo* is Korea's largest newspaper with a daily circulation of about 2.3 million copies? Two other Seoul dailies, *The JoongAng Ilbo* and the *Dong-A Ilbo*, are close behind in readers. *The Wall Street Journal*, by comparison, has a circulation of about two million copies. English-language newspapers published in Seoul include *The Korea Herald*, *The Korea Times* and *The Seoul Times*. The previously mentioned Korean-language dailies also publish English-language editions.

paper, if possible in English and Hangeul (the Korean script).

If traveling on your own, the key is to get directions based on landmarks. For example, to proceed from a subway station: "Take exit 3,

TAKE**5** DAVID A. MASON'S TOP FIVE
SEOUL CITY MOUNTAINS

David A. Mason is a Professor of Korean Tourism at Seoul's Kyung Hee University, and a researcher on the religious character of Korea's mountains. A U.S. citizen, he has lived in Korea for 25 years, and has authored six books on Korean culture and tourism, including *Spirit of the Mountains* and *Passage to Korea*. His popular website on sacred Korean mountains and their spirits can be found at www.san-shin.org. The suffix "san" means "mountain" in Korean.

1. Inwang-san of Jongno-gu and Seodaemun-gu
The sacred "White Tiger" crags looming west of Gyeongbokgung Palace are named the Benevolent King Mountain, and have been the key feature of Seoul's spiritual geography ever since human beings have lived here. It's a great little mountain to hike over in just a couple of hours, offering some of the best views of the downtown skyscrapers beyond the palaces. It is also host to a wonderful complex of Buddhist temples and shamanic shrines that contain profound religious artworks worthy of viewing on repeated visits.

2. Samgak-san in Gangbuk-gu
The "Three Horns," Insu-bong, Baekun-dae and Manggyeong-dae, are mighty and impressive peaks that have always served as the capital's spiritual guardians. Currently part of the Bukhan-san National Park, they are Korea's most popular destination for mountain-hikers and rock-climbers, and host to more than a dozen fantastic Buddhist temples and national-shamanic shrines.

turn right as you leave, go two blocks until you see a Safeway, then look for the green sign." If you get lost, try asking someone for help using the name of your destination rather than its street address.

3. Dobong-san in Dobong-gu

Relatively remote but always worth a visit, this is an amazing set of cliffs and peaks extremely popular with hikers, photographers and picnickers. It is home to several dozen varied religious institutions and sacred sites, as well as some really wonderful artworks including a gigantic statue of Dangun, Korea's Founding-King.

4. Surak-san and Bulam-san in Nowon-gu

These two mountains are really one huge hikeable-ridgeline with sharp craggy peaks that can be seen from all over northeastern Seoul. They have recently become easily accessed from several different metro-train lines, and are deservedly rising in popularity due to their awesome and challenging beauty. They feature dozens of fascinating Buddhist temples both within Seoul's borders and just outside of them.

5. Gwanak-san in Gwanak-gu

These dry rocky crags form the center of Seoul's southern border, and are incredibly popular with weekend-hiker crowds. Mt. Gwanak features the cliff-top Yeonju-am Buddhist shrine, one of the most photogenic sites anywhere, and many other vibrant temples well worth a visit.

TAKE 5 FIVE LEADING SEOUL
UNIVERSITIES

Seoul is a leader in Asia and world-wide for post-secondary education, and many people from other regions of South Korea move to the capital to study. There are dozens of universities, colleges and technical schools in Seoul, and lately, an increasing number of international students. While it is difficult to objectively measure the "best" universities, the following institutions typically rank among the leaders.

1. **Seoul National University.** According to the *Times Higher Education Supplement* 2009 survey, SNU ranks number 47 worldwide. Entrance to SNU is notoriously competitive, and the school's graduates populate the upper echelons of South Korea's top corporations and government institutions. The university, which was founded in 1946, temporarily relocated to Busan during the Korean War. In addition to its role as training ground for the nation's elite, SNU has a strong international orientation and is a high profile research institution.

2. **Korea Advanced Institute of Science and Technology (KAIST).** KAIST was founded in Seoul in 1971 as the country's first graduate institution devoted to science and engineering education and research. KAIST is no longer located in the capital, having moved to the city of Daejeon in 1989. A highly competitive institution, it played a key role in the rise of the Korean auto, chemical and semi-conductor industries in the 1980s.

3. **Yonsei University.** The oldest private university in Korea, Yonsei was established by Christian missionaries in 1885. An important research institution, Yonsei has nearly 30,000 students, 3,500 faculty and 19 graduate schools.

4. **Korea University.** Founded in 1905, KU has 35,000 students and a picturesque campus. It is particularly strong in the humanities and Asian studies, and is known for its role in preserving and fostering Korean culture.

5. **Ewha Womans University.** Founded by a Methodist missionary in 1886, Ewha was a pioneer in women's education in Korea and today enrolls 20,000 graduate and undergraduate students. The name "Ewha" was bestowed by Emperor Gojong in 1887, and means "pear blossoms." In 1946, following Korea's liberation, Ewha became the nation's first accredited four-year university.

The Splendid Subway

Seoul's subway debuted in 1974 and is fast, safe, clean and inexpensive. With over 400 stations, it will get you virtually anywhere in the city you want to go. Many subway stations have restrooms and lockers, and the larger stations are usually connected to underground shopping areas. Some stations incorporate whimsical design elements including fish tanks, murals and sculptures, making them worth the trip itself. Best of all, the system is easy to use and all of the signs and announcements are in both Korean and English.

Virgin Vacations ranks the Seoul system sixth (between Tokyo and New York) in its "Top 11" underground transit systems worldwide. Virgin notes the Seoul subway's "beautiful architecture," as well as its spectacular expansion in recent years. The Seoul subway has nine lines and logs more than 8.1 million passenger trip daily; during peak operating hours, the average interval between trains is two and a half to three minutes. Seoul's subway ranks among the world's busiest, trailing Tokyo and Moscow, but ranking ahead of New York City, Mexico City and Paris in ridership.

The general adult fare is 1,000 won (less than one U.S. dollar) for the first 10 kilometers, and an additional 100 won each additional 5 kilometers. Senior citizens and the disabled ride free. Seoul's subway connects to surrounding cities like Incheon (including the airport) and Suwon, and also links to inter-city rail and bus stations. The Seoul CityPass and SeoulCityPass+ are rechargeable transportation cards

Did you know. . .

that on May 22, 2007, line 2 of Seoul's subway system carried its 30 billionth passenger? The system records about two billion passenger trips yearly. Prior to the introduction of the reusable single journey subway ticket in 2009, the Seoul subway network issued more than 450 million paper tickets annually.

which can be used on the subway, buses and the Seoul City Tour Bus. The "plus" card can also be used to purchase goods in T-money member stores, as well as for discounts at various attractions.

One tip: Pay attention to which exit you need to take when leaving the station to get to your destination. Subway maps are available at many places in Seoul, as well as in person and online through the Seoul City and Korea tourism organizations, and from the Seoul Metropolitan Rapid Transit Corporation (www.smrt.co.kr/Eng/index.jsp).

Riding the Seoul subway is a bargain. The following 2010 survey of systems worldwide is for a one-way adult cash fare using the fewest possible zones (where applicable).

City	Local currency	U.S. dollars
Beijing	2.0 yuan	$0.29
Seoul	**1,000 won**	**$0.87**
Moscow	26 rubles	$0.87
Rio de Janeiro	2.8 reals	$1.55
Tokyo	160 yen (up to 6 km)	$1.75
New York	$2.25	$2.25
Stockholm	20 kroner (basic, one zone)	$2.77
Berlin	2.1 euroS (one zone)	$2.84
Toronto	$3.00 CDN	$2.89
London	4 pounds	$6.08

Sources: Beijing Subway Corp. Seoul Metropolitan Rapid Transit Corp., Moscow Metro, Tokyo Metro Co., Ltd., Metropolitan Transportation Authority-New York City Transit (MTA-NYC Transit), Toronto Transit Commission, Transport for London, Metro Rio, Stockholm Metro, BVG.

Buses

There are approximately 10,000 buses in Seoul, and over 4.5 million trips taken daily. While the bus system may seem confusing, there are some general rules and most buses are color-coded:

- Blue buses are wide ranging and run between the most popular locations in Seoul (1,000 won).

- Green buses run between major subway and bus transfer points (1,000 won).
- Red buses connect Seoul with its satellite cities (1,600 won).
- Yellow buses connect subway stations and major bus transfer points, and also hit many major attractions in the central city (800 won).
- Green buses with only two-digits are neighborhood buses (700 won).

The official Seoul city government site, www.seoul.go.kr, has a very useful "bus map" in English which lets people map out which buses they need to take to get from point A to point B. Finally, if you are using a T-money card, which entitles you to a small discount, place it on the panel as you enter *and* leave the bus.

Taxis

- Normal taxis cost 2,400 won for the first 2 kilometers (1.2 miles). A 20 percent surcharge is added for travel between midnight and 4 a.m.
- Deluxe taxis (black) are 4,500 won for the first 3 kilometers (1.8 miles), and there is no midnight surcharge.
- Jumbo taxis (black) are available by call and are comparable to deluxe taxis in price, but with an extra 1,000 won dispatch fee.
- International taxis (orange) cost 20 percent more than normal taxis, and cater to foreigners. There are currently 120 international taxis in Seoul, but that number is expected to double. They can be reserved and chartered at www.internationaltaxi.co.kr.

Seoul City Tour Bus

One ticket allows the rider to get on and off the bus at multiple locations, and there are downtown tours, palace tours and night-time tours. Departure points include Gwanghwamun subway (near Gyeongbokgung Palace), Seoul Station and Yongsan Station. There are single and double-decker buses, and group discounts are available. Visit www.visitseoul.net for more information, or call 02-777-6090 (the "02" is not needed in Seoul).

Incheon International Airport

Incheon International Airport, which opened in 2001, was named "World's Best Airport" in 2009 by Skytrax, which bases its rankings on customer surveys drawn from 190 airports worldwide. Incheon International features numerous high tech amenities, great food and shopping, and an out-of-this world observation deck. It is also home to the Korean Culture Museum (operated in cooperation with the National Museum of Korea) as well as other cultural galleries and exhibitions. The airport is well connected to Seoul, and there are plenty of easily accessed buses, shuttles, taxis, and limos, as well as a rail link. Visit www.airport.kr/eng/ for more information. Seoul's second airport, Gimpo, is used primarily for domestic flights.

Key Weblinks and Numbers

(For a further list of sites devoted to arts, entertainment and culture in Seoul, including newspapers and magazine sites, see the end of the "Arts and Entertainment" chapter).

Seoul City Tourism

www.visitseoul.net

Part of the Seoul Metropolitan Government, the site has plentiful information on accommodations, food, tours, day-trips, shopping and transportation. There is also material on events, activities, museums and sights along the themes of traditional, modern and outdoor Seoul, as well as links to many other sites. Call DASAN Seoul call center 120(9) from Seoul.

Seoul Convention Bureau

www.miceseoul.com

The Seoul Convention Bureau is a division of the Seoul Tourism Organization and part of Seoul Metropolitan Government. The site features a venue finder, as well as promotions and information about Seoul for meeting planners and tourism professionals.

Seoul Metropolitan Government

www.seoul.go.kr

Lots of material on Seoul for tourists, businesspeople and locals. Includes activities, events and news.

Seoul Global Center

www.global.seoul.go.kr

Useful information on business and daily life for foreigners living in Seoul. Open regular business hours. Locally, from Seoul: 1688-0120.

Korea Tourism Organization (KTO)

www.visitkorea.or.kr.

Seoul naturally figures heavily in the KTO site, which is a must if you are traveling outside of the capital city.

Republic of Korea Official Website

www.korea.net/

A lively site with material on Korean culture, government, economy and other topics. Plenty of stats, current events and practical information.

KBS World

www.world.kbs.co.kr/english/

Korean Broadcasting System in English. Lots of Korean and foreign news as well as arts, entertainment and travel coverage.

Korea Tourism Tourist Information Center: Dial 1330. Very useful if you find yourself in a jam, or just plain puzzled. The service is open 24 hours daily and staffed by Korean, English, Japanese and Chinese speakers. From a cell phone, dial "02" before the number.

Dasan Call Center

A one-stop call center for information on daily life in Seoul. Service is available in English and some other languages. Dial 120 from Seoul.

BBB (Before Babel Brigade Service). Interpretation provided by volunteers from 17 countries. From Seoul: 1588-5644.

Weather

Seoul's humid continental climate can be fickle. It can also pack a stronger punch than one might imagine of a city positioned at 37 degrees north latitude – about the same as San Francisco and Athens. While Seoul is set squarely in the temperate zone, each of the city's four seasons can bring with it extremes of pleasure (and sometimes pain).

Winters, while dry, can be cold and windy; spring is pleasant and ushers in a vivid explosion of flower blossoms; summer is typically humid and can bring heavy rains. Finally, autumn rewards generously with cloudless, sunny days and crisp, cool nights set against a resplendent backdrop of colorful foliage.

Seoul's varied weather conditions can be explained, in part, by Korea's position at the far eastern tip of the Asian landmass, which brings cold high-pressure systems from Siberia in the winter and moist maritime Pacific air masses in the summer. Seoul's annual variation in temperature is similar to that of other continental climes, although the city gets 72 percent of its yearly precipitation in only four months – June through September.

That said, Seoul enjoys downright pleasant weather for much of the year compared to the abuses that Mother Nature hurls at other East Asian cities in the Philippines, Taiwan, and Japan. Winter in Seoul might be chilly, but the city sees only about 27 centimeters (10.6 inches) of snowfall yearly (though much more drapes the nearby mountains, making for lovely views). Likewise, as much as home appliance stores see a near stampede of air-conditioner shoppers every May and June, city slickers need only endure seven "tropical nights" (nights when the mercury doesn't dip below 25 C) each summer. But Koreans don't much care to sweat, or shiver, and most hotels, theaters, restaurants and even subway platforms are kept comfortable year-round with air conditioners and heaters.

Climate doesn't get Seoulites down, and they employ a variety of measures, both ancient and modern, in coping with the city's four distinct seasons. In a city always longing for something new and "dynamic," the whimsical behavior of Seoul's weather is a perfect fit.

AT A GLANCE

- Warmest month – August: 29.5° C (85° F) average high; 22.1° C (72° F) average low.
- Coldest month – January: 1.6° C (35° F) average high; -6.1° C (21° F) average low.
- Sunniest month – October: average 200.5 hours of sunshine.
- Windiest months – March and April: average wind speed 10.4 kph (6.5 mph).
- Rainiest month – August: average 348 mm (13.7 inches) of rain.
- Driest month – January: average 21.6 mm (0.85 inches) precipitation.
- Most humid month: July – average 79.8 percent humidity.

Source: Korea Meteorological Administration

Did you know. . .

that until the 1950s, the Han River, which runs through Seoul, remained frozen for about 80 days each winter? Before refrigeration became common, ice was "harvested" from the Han to use in preserving fish and other perishables during the warmer months. In years gone by, winter recreation in Seoul included ice hockey on the Han and skiing on Mount Namsan. Since the 1990s, iced-over conditions on the Han have lasted for only about 10 days each winter.

WINTER AND SUMMER
TEMPERATURES AROUND SOUTH KOREA

Daily average January and August temperatures (in degrees Celsius with degrees Fahrenheit in parentheses)

	January	August	Location
Seoul	-2.5 (27.5° F)	25.4 (77.7° F)	Midway up peninsula, 40 km/25 mi. from W coast.
Busan	3 (37.4° F)	25.7 (78.3° F)	On SE coast, 327 km/203 mi. SE of Seoul.
Jeju	5.6 (42° F)	26.5 (79.7° F)	Island off Korea's S coast, 453 km/280 mi. S of Seoul.
Gangneung	0.3 (32.5° F)	24.4 (75.9° F)	On NE coast, 210 km/130 mi. NE of Seoul.
Daejeon	-1.9 (28.6° F)	25.5 (77.9° F)	W central interior, 150 km/93 mi. S of Seoul.
Daegu	0.2 (32.4° F)	26.1 (79.0° F)	Inland SE, 236 km/147 mi. SE of Seoul.
Gwangju	0.5 (32.9° F)	26.1 (79.0° F)	Inland SW, 268 km/167 mi. S of Seoul.
Chungju	-4.1 (24.6° F)	24.8 (76.6° F)	Central interior, 115 km/71 mi. SE of Seoul.
Chuncheon	-4.5 (23.9° F)	24.3 (75.7° F)	NE interior, 73 km/45 mi. NE of Seoul.

Source: Korea Meteorological Administration

TAKE 5 METEOROLOGIST KIM SEUNG-BAI'S FIVE MOST CHALLENGING ASPECTS OF FORECASTING SEOUL'S WEATHER

Kim Seung-bai, Senior Meteorologist at the Korea Meteorological Administration in Seoul, was born in the heartland city of Jeonju, North Jeolla Province. He later moved to Seoul, and after obtaining a master's degree in atmospheric sciences from Yonsei University, joined the Korea Meteorological Administration, where he served in the international cooperation division before being promoted to the rank of senior meteorologist.

Mr. Kim's responsibilities include explaining weather forecasts to reporters at media outlets. He has also discussed the weather on TV and radio numerous times himself, and is known for his ability to present difficult scientific information in an easy-to-digest manner.

1. **The Korean Peninsula, where Seoul is located, belongs to the mid-latitudes of the northern hemisphere.** Around here, cold air from the higher latitudes meets hot air from the lower latitudes, causing powerful shifts in weather. The mid-latitudes also have various different kinds of air masses, whose influence fluctuates with the season. On top of this, because 70 percent of the Korean Peninsula is mountainous, we see extreme variations in local weather.

2. **In order to accurately predict the weather, one must first get a clear picture of weather conditions around the peninsula.** Since the Korean Peninsula is surrounded by seas on three sides, however, this is difficult. That's because it is not possible to build weather observatories in the middle of open waters to monitor changes in the weather in real time.

3. **Korea is in an area of prevailing westerly winds, and air currents from China (which lies to the west of Korea) move over the Korean Peninsula and then on toward Japan and out to the Pacific Ocean.** The dry continental air from China changes rapidly as it meets the

water, becoming more humid as it passes over the West Sea (also known as the Yellow Sea). When such air meets the mountains in the interior it gets forced upward, causing localized areas of torrential rain or heavy snow. This phenomenon can occur in such small pockets that it is hard to observe, much less forecast. It is especially challenging to forecast Seoul's weather because it is near the West Sea. Atmospheric conditions, which have already changed out at sea, change again as they run into obstacles like mountains just after moving inland.

4. **Seoul is a megacity with over 10 million people.** The temperature in a megacity, with its abundant tall buildings and dense population, is higher than that of the suburbs due to all the heat that gets discharged from buildings' heating and air conditioning systems, and the huge amount of car exhaust. There is also something we call "Building Wind," which is a disruption to normal wind flow caused by buildings. The complexities of air flow and higher temperatures in a large city are yet another reason why weather changes can be rapid – and extreme.

5. **Koreans think the weather forecast should be 100 percent accurate at all times.** Part of the reason is that they do not fully understand the science of weather forecasting. At times it can rain to the north of the Han River, while the sun is shining south of the river. When we forecast rain for Seoul, people think it will therefore rain in their neighborhood. Since weather is a natural phenomenon, it can behave differently from one area to another. The public's high expectations make the meteorologist's job very tough.

They said it

"The climate is undoubtedly one of the finest and healthiest in the world. Foreigners are not afflicted by any climatic maladies, and European children can be safely brought up in every part of the peninsula. July, August, and sometimes the first half of September, are hot and rainy, but the heat is so tempered by sea breezes that exercise is always possible. For nine months of the year the skies are generally bright, and a Korean winter is absolutely superb, with its still atmosphere, its bright, blue, unclouded sky, its extreme dryness without asperity, and its crisp frosty nights. From the middle of September till the end of June, there are neither extremes of heat nor cold to guard against."

– British travel writer Isabella Lucy Bird describing Korea's climate in her 1898 book *Korea and Her Neighbours*.

EXTREME WEATHER

Seoul can get pretty hot, and it can also get pretty cold. Much the same can be said for its potential for wind and rain. Bear in mind, however, that what follows are the exceptions, not the rules.

- **Highest temperature on record:** 38.4° C (101° F) on July 24, 1994.
- **Lowest temperature on record:** -23.1° C (-6° F) on December 31, 1927.
- **Highest wind speed:** 113 kph (70 mph) on September 26, 1995.
- **Most rainfall in one day:** 354.7 mm (14 inches) on August 2, 1920.
- **Most snowfall in one day:** 310 mm (12.2 inches) on March 24, 1922.

Sources: Korea Meteorological Administration

Did you know. . .

that Seoul's biggest snowfall in recent memory was a January 4, 2010 blanketing that left 26 centimeters (10 inches) of the white stuff on the ground? It was the deepest snowfall since modern meteorological observations began in 1937. The accumulation was about the same as Seoul typically receives over the course of an entire winter.

Did you know. . .

that what Europeans and North Americans call "radiant floor heating" is in fact a traditional method of heating Korean homes? In olden times, heat from the kitchen wood stove was carried to other parts of the dwelling through channels beneath the floor stones. This method of under-floor heating is known as *ondol*, and it produces an evenly distributed heat free of drafts, which makes sitting – and sleeping – on the floor quite comfortable. Many newer Korean homes still employ *ondol*, although the water-filled pipes under the floor are now heated by electricity or gas rather than fire.

TYPHOONS

During the early summer rainy season, from one to three typhoons typically descend on the Korean Peninsula from the South Pacific. Often taking a westerly approach from Japan, they can pack heavy rains and gale-force winds. In 2002, the most powerful storm in recent memory, Typhoon Rusa, dumped up to 900 mm (35.4 inches) of rain on parts of Korea over a two-day period, causing major destruction. A year later, Typhoon Maemi struck with winds up to 215 kph (134 mph).

Storms of such intensity are rare, and Korea's southern and coastal regions, including number two city Busan, generally bear the brunt of these hurricanes' fury. Seoul typically escapes real damage at the hands of typhoons, and for city residents tropical storms are more inconvenient than dangerous.

Did you know. . .

that the 1988 Seoul Summer Olympics was mostly held in autumn? To allow athletes to compete without being drenched by summer rains, Seoul Olympics organizers pushed back the dates of the 24th Olympiad to September 17 through October 3. Korea's coming-out bash marked only the fourth Summer Games not to take place in the summer – and the last whose opening ceremony took place in broad daylight!

TAKE 5 — TOP FIVE TIPS FOR SURVIVING SUMMER IN SEOUL

When the heat is on—the summer heat, that is—folks in Seoul will pull something from the bagful of tricks they've come to depend on to cool off. Some of these survival strategies date back centuries, to a time when most Koreans lived on farms and relied on their wits, and the wisdom of the ages, to stay cool.

1. *Yiyeol-chiyeol* 이열치열 ("using heat to pacify heat")

Oriental medical theory contends that a person's body cannot properly release its heat during hot weather. By ingesting hot foods, however, you open the skin's pores to allow body heat to escape. Hot foods known to warm the inner body, such as chicken and ginseng, are highly regarded for coping with hot weather. This explains the popularity of eating energy-replenishing dishes like *samgyetang* (chicken-and-ginseng soup) on *sambok* days, the three hottest of summer. Lines form outside Seoul's *samgyetang* restaurants on these days, so get there early!

2. Bamboo Mats

When the mercury goes up, the bamboo mats come down from storage. Bamboo stays cooler than the air temperature, and keeps a person dry and comfortable by repelling humidity. Such mats find a place not just on floors, but also on car seats, beds, and sofas. A variation is the *jukbuin*, a long hard pillow made of loosely woven bamboo strands that people "hug" to stay cool. Men lovingly embrace such pillows, whose name literally means "bamboo wife."

3. Ramie and Linen Clothing

In the days before LG and Samsung, Korean commoners' "air conditioners" were clothes made of stiff, rough ramie fabric. (Only the aristocrats wore linen). The advantages of these fabrics in hot, sticky weather still hold true today: they wick away moisture, don't stick to the body, are super-breathable, and feel cool to the touch. They are also resilient to water, so they can be washed often without damage. In recent years, designers have introduced contemporary ramie and linen styles to appeal to foreigners and the younger generation.

4. Horror Films

Most Korean horror movies are released in the summertime, a season when TV dramas and entertainment shows also scare up horror-related themes. What's the point, you ask? It's believed that the spine-tingling thrills, chills—and goose bumps—you get watching zombies, ghosts, and other spooks literally "chills" people out and helps them forget about the heat for a while.

5. Sprinklers and Fountains

When the going gets sweaty, the sweaty get going . . . to the nearest water sprinkler! In what could rightly be called a Seoul civic priority, serious sprinklers have sprung up like mushrooms after the rain in the city's parks and civic spaces. There's even one right outside City Hall. When a heat wave strikes, normally docile tykes are given full license to dash and splash through the large fountains. Seoul's 200-plus sprinklers spring to life around April each year, with some offering a bonus: music-and-light shows in the morning and evening. Other places to dip one's feet include Cheonggyecheon Stream and Gwanghwamun Square.

6. A Han River Cruise

A thoroughly enjoyable way to beat the heat is an evening cruise on the Han River. A river jaunt complete with cold Hite beers, a dinner buffet, and a karaoke bar is a sure way to cool down and take the edge off.

CLIMATE CHANGE

Seoul's weather data presents clear evidence of a local warming trend over the past century. Seoul's average temperature climbed to 13.5° C (56° F) during the 1997 to 2007 period from 10.6° C (51.1° F) in 1908-1917; the number of "tropical days" above 25° C (77° F) climbed to 37 yearly from 31. Meanwhile, the number of below-freezing days has fallen to 86 a year from a whopping 129 a century ago.

Sure enough, springtime blossoms come later, arriving around April 5 now as opposed to April 18, which was recorded as recently as the 1958-1967 period. Autumn foliage now hits its peak around November 8, compared to October 23 forty years ago. Climate change has also brought more – and heavier – rains than in the past. Not all the news is grim: Among those poised to prosper from warmer temps are Korea's fruit farmers. At the Agriculture Research Center for Climate Change in Jeju Island, researchers have begun to experiment with growing such subtropical and tropical crops as okra, artichokes and sugar beets.

TAKE5 JANUARY AND JULY
AVERAGE LOWS AND HIGHS
FOR FIVE CITIES WORLDWIDE

	January	July
Seoul	-6.1/1.6° C (21/35° F)	21.8/28.8° C (71/84° F)
New York	-3.3/3.3° C (26/38° F)	19.4/28.8° C (67/84° F)
Paris	1/6° C (33.8/42.8° F)	15/25° C (59/77° F)
Hong Kong	14/18.6° C (57.2/65.5° F)	26.7/31.3° C (80/88.3° F)
Sydney	19/26° C (66/79° F)	9/16° C (49/61° F)

Sources: KMA, New York City & Co., Paris Convention and Visitors' Bureau, Hong Kong Observatory (City of Hong Kong), City of Sydney.

YELLOW DUST

Spring is welcome in the capital for its incredible flowers and greenery, but it has one negative: *hwangsa*, or yellow dust. It's not a made-in-Korea phenomena. The dust is the product of the deserts of western China, Mongolia and Kazakhstan which kick up clouds of fine soil particles. As winds move over China's industrial heartland, they gather up and carry various pollutants which sometimes fall on the Korean Peninsula as a fine mist of yellow sand.

High levels of yellow dust can potentially pose a threat to the elderly, young children and those with respiratory problems like asthma. As such, Korea's weather and environmental agencies monitor conditions during the yellow dust "season" and provide warnings to those who are at high risk. Fortunately, for the vast majority of people, seasonal dust is an occasional annoyance and not a real concern. Korean authorities have sought to combat the problem by funding tree-planting projects across China and Mongolia's arid reaches. Yellow dust episodes usually run their course by mid-May.

EARTHQUAKES

Unlike its neighbors Japan and China, Korea is at low risk from earthquakes. Since wide-scale measurement began in 1978, an average of 20 quakes have been recorded yearly. The vast majority of these tremors, however, measured less than 3.0 on the Richter scale and were small enough that they were not felt. In addition to earthquake sensors, the Korea Meteorological Administration has a tsunami monitoring system in place. Monitors on an island in the East Sea 130 kilometers (100 miles) from the South Korean coast automatically transmit data to 80 institutes nationwide.

THE RAINY SEASON

The heat starts building up in May. As spring's mild, pleasant days increasingly give way to blazing sunshine and high humidity, office workers don short-sleeve dress shirts and that old standby—the paper fan—is deployed to provide a little relief. By mid-June, staying cool and dry has become a major goal.

Just when the heat threatens to agitate people into defecting to North Korea, the tension breaks. The skies open up for and the mercury drops. As streets and sidewalks turn to rivulets, moving splotches of color punctuate the streetscape — small children decked out in bright-yellow raincoats and rain boots leaping across (and sometimes into) puddles. Umbrella vendors do a brisk business, all the more so since the accompanying winds lay to waste all but the best-built parasols. *Jangma*, the rainy season, has arrived in Seoul.

Referred to as the "monsoon season," the annual rain front traditionally arrives on the Korean Peninsula in late June and lingers until mid-July. The result of a mid-air collision between the cold *Okhotsk* high-pressure system and a warm North Pacific atmospheric system, *jangma* (said to derive from *dangma*, which means "long water") dumps some 340 millimeters (13.4 inches) of rain — about a quarter of yearly rainfall — on the city. Up to 200 mm (7.9 inches) can fall in one day, turning roads into rivers as sewers are overwhelmed. These rains also inundate the rice paddies, something of a blessing to farmers of the country's staple grain.

For years, Korea's national weather agency would announce the official starting date of the rainy season up to a month before it arrived. But it ended this practice around 2007 after being pelted with com-

Did you know. . .

that some weather stations serving Seoul include special indexes in their reports that give viewers advice from a meteorological perspective on matters like whether to do their laundry or get the car washed over the next 24 hours? Known as *jisu*, these indexes also give a score on the likelihood of getting sound sleep that night, or whether one should exercise or apply skin cream the next day.

They said it

"The heat of the inland cities such as Seoul causes many western residents to seek relief on the seashore or in the mountains, where the temperature is more moderate. Resorts are abundant and readily accessible."

— From a 1951 issue of *The Voice of Korea*, published by the Washington, D.C.-based Korean Affairs Institute.

plaints over inaccurately forecasting the start or end of the wet period. Nowadays, Korea Meteorological Administration officials wait until just a few days before the rain front arrives to issue a statement.

Weather experts say that efforts to define a distinct rainy season have been stymied lately because the North Pacific high pressure system fails to reach as far south as the Korean Peninsula, instead heading due west to inland China. The result, for Korea, is no clear seasonal rain front and a longer rainy period taking in both July and August.

During the cloudy, rainy weather, Seoulites search out ways to stay dry and sane. It's a time when cinemas fill up, coffee shops brim with customers, and bookstores do a brisk business. There's still plenty to see and do, even outside; just have an umbrella at the ready.

Weblinks

Korea Meteorological Administration (KMA)

http://web.kma.go.kr/eng

The KMA site offers local digital forecasts for all cities and areas in South Korea. It also provides current conditions, mid-term and long-range forecasts, and severe weather warnings.

Urban Geography

Situated along the Han River and home to 26 mountains, Seoul is unique among world capitals. And with a population of 10.5 million people, and more than double that number in the capital region, Seoul ranks as one of the world's largest urban areas.

Seoul's history stretches back millennia and combines the old and the new, the traditional and the high-tech. It embodies a firm embrace of the present and a reverence for the past. Korea's capital for over 600 years, Seoul is home to two UNESCO World Heritage Sites: Jongmyo Shrine and Changdeokgung Palace. And yet, at the same time, Seoul has been designated the 2010 World Design Capital. Indeed, this is a city where palaces and hanok (traditional housing) mix with skyscrapers and some of the world's most innovative architecture.

As a result of its explosive growth in the decades following the Korean War, Seoul is one of the planet's most contemporary—even futuristic—cities. It is a place that has reinvented itself. Seoul's inclusion in the pantheon of the world's great cities has produced with it an understanding that quality-of-life and sustainability issues are crucial to its future. It continues to add green spaces, improve leisure and recreation facilities and upgrade cultural properties. Every year seems to bring a new city landmark – Gwanghwamun Square (which debuted in 2009) and Dongdaemun Design Plaza (opening in 2011) are just two of many. This is a city that believes everything and anything is possible.

They said it

GEOMANTIC SEOUL

The surrounding mountains and the city's Han River location have served Seoul well, providing the city with natural, inland defense and a coastal transportation system. However, it was geomancy, or *pungsu-jiri*, and not geography that was the chief consideration in the placement of the capital.

According to geomantic principles, natural features exude an inner energy that influences human fortunes. Building a capital in an auspicious locale was considered essential to securing its prosperity and longevity. Bounded to the east by mountains resembling a blue dragon, to the west by a ridge shaped like a white tiger, and crossed in front by a major waterway, Seoul was an obvious choice.

Doseon, a ninth-century Buddhist monk and master geomancer, predicted that Seoul's prime location would make it the site of a dynasty that would enjoy a 500-year reign. His prophecy, for the most part, came true. The Yi or Joseon Kingdom was founded in 1392, and endured until 1910.

GEOLOGICAL ORIGINS

The Korean Peninsula was formed by violent prehistoric volcanic activity, plate movement and uplift, and erosion. More than 60 percent of Korea is covered with granite and gneiss (a metamorphic rock). These rocks are often seen as the bare peaks and summits of Korea's many mountains.

The gneiss in Korea is between 1,800 and 2,500 million years old, while the granite is a mere 161 million years old. The constant upheavals of these ancient rocks and their subsequent erosion by the elements led the ancients to describe Korea as geumsu-gangsan, or "river and mountains embroidered on silk."

SEOUL BOASTS . . .

- 479 post offices
- 106 museums
- 95 embassies
- 5, 203 public restrooms
- 15,602,387 books in 85 libraries
- 883 kindergartens
- 2,409 parks
- 8,092 km (5,057 miles) of paved roads
- 36 rivers and streams (240 kilometers or 150 miles)
- 24 Han River bridges
- 24 tunnels (longest: Hongjimun Tunnel at 1.9 kilometers or 1.2 miles)
- 5,414 public buses using compressed natural gas

SEOUL PLAYS IN . . .

- 84 sports complexes
- 100 gymnasiums
- 51 tennis court facilities
- 11 ice rinks
- 87 swimming pools
- 61 baseball/soccer fields
- 1,595 golf practice ranges

GWANGHWAMUN SQUARE

The square opened in 2009 on the site of what had been the Joseon Kingdom's main thoroughfare. This is where the royal offices were

Cheonggyecheon –
A Waterway Reborn

For centuries Cheonggyecheon Stream was a vital artery running through the heart of Seoul. By the post-war era, however, it had become heavily polluted and was viewed as a barrier to the city's modernization and growth. In the 1950s, the stream was paved over and the shabby housing around it demolished. The 1970s brought an elevated expressway over Cheonggyecheon, and almost all traces of the stream were eradicated.

The obliteration of Cheonggyecheon made sense at the time, but by the 1990s it was clear that Seoul would not be sustainable if every inch of it was to be given over to roads and high rises. The administration of then-mayor Lee Myung-bak (now the President of South Korea) made restoring Cheonggyecheon a top priority.

A $384-million reconstruction project, which included removing the expressway, was completed in 2005. The six kilometer (3.5 mile) stream is now a popular pedestrian site attracting some 100,000 visitors daily. Large flat stones allow pedestrians to traverse the banks of the stream, and the project also features paths, bridges, murals and sculptures. At nighttime colorful lighting further accentuates this remarkable recovery.

Cheonggyecheon is an attraction for all seasons. In summer, people remove their shoes and cool their feet in the water, while in December Christmas lights are a big draw. There is also the Cheonggyecheon Museum featuring exhibits and information on the stream and its restoration.

Cheonggyecheon's refurbishment has not only improved Seoul's downtown area by creating a prime leisure space, it has also had an environmental impact. Summer temperatures near the stream are up to five degrees C. cooler than in other parts of the city, and biological diversity has increased with a rise in fish, bird and insect populations.

Good places to start an exploration of Cheonggyecheon are at Cheonggyecheon Plaza (at the western end of the stream walk), or at the Cheonggyecheon Museum (on the eastern extremity). In addition to the stream itself, attractions along the way include the Seoul Flea Market and Dongdaemun Market.

found, and the king himself would promenade in the area. These days, the vehicles move faster and the buildings are taller, but the district still represents Seoul's historic heart.

Gwanghwamun Square lies in front of Gwanghwamun Gate, the entrance to Gyeongbokgung Palace. The square was created by reclaiming six lanes of traffic and transforming them into a multi-purpose area dedicated to Korea and its history.

The square measures 557 meters (1,825 feet) in length, and its flowing water is perfect for wading during the warmer months. The space is packed with symbols and associations: The 220,000 flowers present at its debut commemorated the 220,000 days from Seoul becoming the capital in 1394 up to the plaza's unveiling.

The floor of the square's waterway is composed of 617 stones recording major events from the advent of the Joseon Kingdom in 1392 to current times. In keeping with the water theme, an elaborate fountain commemorates Korean Admiral Yi Sun-sin's victory in repelling foreign invasions in the 1500s. There is also an imposing statue of the intrepid admiral, as well as one of the legendary King Sejong.

Gwanghwamun Square is often used for concerts and festivals, and was designed to provide Seoul a grand civic space on the order of the National Mall in Washington D.C. or the Champs Elysées in Paris. It is a place for all seasons, featuring ice skating in winter and splashing water in summer.

Did you know...

that South Korea's largest mall is Times Square in southwestern Seoul? The mega-mall debuted in September 2009 and in the 100 days following its opening logged over 20 million visits and $240 million in sales. The Lotte World complex in Jamsil, which opened in the 1980s, is generally considered South Korea's first large scale mall.

NAMSAN MOUNTAIN

The 262-meter (860 foot) tall Namsan Mountain lies at the center of Seoul. At one time it was on the city's outskirts, hence its name, which literally means "South Mountain."

Namsan Mountain is surrounded by a huge park of pine and Mongolian oak trees, the foliage of which provide a peaceful respite for Seoul's ten million plus residents, as well as a habitat for many birds and small animals. It is nature in the heart of one of the world's busiest cities.

During the Joseon era, smoke and fire beacons were located on the mountain's summit as part of a nationwide communication system. In 1969, a TV and radio tower, now known as N Seoul Tower, was constructed, making it the highest point in Seoul. The tower facility was opened to the public in 1980, and now boasts two revolving restaurants, and a high tech observatory.

The nighttime vista from the 237 meter (777 foot) N Seoul Tower is spectacular. (And, even if nature calls while you are up high, you can visit the beautifully appointed "Sky Restroom.")

At the tower's base thousands of small locks are attached to fences. Young couples come to N Seoul with a lock, write their names on it, and then secure the lock in place as a symbol of their eternal love.

Transportation to the summit of Namsan is limited to buses and cable cars, and, of course, that old standby, shoe leather. The Namsan Circle Route Bus stops at several points, including Chungmuro station and the National Theater of Korea, before heading up the hill. These yellow buses run every five to eight minutes until midnight, and cost 800 won (roughly 80 cents). Another strategy is to take a cab to the parking lot below the summit, and then walk the remaining way. For exercise buffs, there is a seven kilometer (four mile) walking path that traverses the mountain.

The Namsan cable car is an enduring tradition and provides wonderful views; a roundtrip ticket is 7,000 won for adults and 4,500 won for children. Getting to the cable car is now a cinch with the 2009 opening of the Namsan Oreumi, an inclined outdoor elevator. The free Oreumi is similar to a funicular and ideal for those with mobility problems. It travels from the plaza near Namsan Tunnel 3 up the side of the mountain to the cable car station parking lot.

The observatory and restaurants are open until 11 pm or midnight most days.

DEPARTMENT STORES

Retail is insanely competitive in South Korea, and Seoul's department stores are an important part of the mix. Their prices are higher than those of the markets, but the major department stores are beautifully designed, carry a vast selection of the very latest styles and have excellent customer service.

Shinsegae

The grand old dame of Korean department stores, Shinsegae opened in 1930 and is Seoul's longest running such emporium. It sells everything from gourmet foods to perfume to the latest designer togs. The 14-floor main Seoul store was upgraded and redesigned in 2006 and is located in Chungmuro, across from the Bank of Korea and Central Post Office, and not far from Namdaemun Market and Myeong-dong. Shinsegae is between the Hoehyeon and Myeong-dong stops on line 4. Tel. 02 1588-1234. department.shinsegae.com.

Lotte

The chain operates 22 stores across Korea, including seven in Seoul alone. The main store in Myeong-dong is well known for its superlative selection, as well as its décor and exceptional restaurant floor. The store is near the Lotte Hotel and the Lotte Young Plaza shopping mall, and is a 10-minute walk from its competitor, Shinsegae. Euljiro 1-ga on subway line 2 provides a direct entrance to the store. Tel. 02 771-2500. www.lotteshopping.com. Other popular Lotte locations in Seoul include Jamsil and Gangnam.

Galleria

Galleria's brightly lit shimmering façade on Rodeo Street is a beacon to well-heeled shoppers in trendy Apgujeong. Lots of top name brands are on offer in a stylish environment. Apgujeong station, line 3. Tel. 02 3449-4114. dept.galleria.co.kr.

Hyundai

Foreigners are familiar with Hyundai the car, but in South Korea Hyundai is a giant conglomerate with a major retail arm. The flagship store in Apgujeong is a massive emporium with six floors, two subterranean levels and a rooftop garden. Apgujeong station, line 3. Tel. 02 547-2233. www.ehyundai.com.

AK Plaza

The four-store chain belongs to the Aekyung Group, which manufactures detergents, cosmetics, and other personal items. The flagship store is in Guro-gu in southwestern Seoul, south of the river. Guro station, line 1. Tel. 02 818-1000. www.akplaza.com.

NAMDAEMUN MARKET

If it exists, you can find it at Namdaemun. Located in the heart of Seoul, the market stocks everything from camping equipment, children's clothes, underwear and *hanbok* (traditional Korean attire), to watches, cookware, ginseng, accessories and jewelry.

Vendors are grouped by category, making comparison shopping easy. One example is the entire section devoted to eyeglasses; the styles are the very latest, and the prices, by North American and European standards, stunningly low. Many of the market's wholesale arcades are open all night, and there are plenty of casual spots to grab a bite to eat. Even if you don't buy anything, Namdaemun is a wonderful place to explore, and should rank high on any "must-visit" list while in Seoul.

The market is centrally located, not far from Myeong-dong (which lies to the east), Seoul Station (to the south) and City Hall (to the north). On Namdaemun's western flank is Sungnyemun (Namdaemun Gate), National Treasure No. 1. The easiest access to the market is by Hoehyeon station on subway line 4. Much of the market is closed on Sundays.

TAKE5 FIVE SEOUL
MARKETS

In addition to the biggies, Namdaemun and Dongdaemun, there are numerous markets throughout Seoul selling all manner of products.

1. **Noryangjin Fisheries Wholesale Market.** Established in 1927, this is the largest marine market in Seoul. Purchasers bid on fish from one a.m. until dawn, but the more than 250 small shops and restaurants scattered throughout the market are open 24-hours. Many of these stores have large tanks filled with colorful and unique fish. Choose the fish you want, and the owner will deftly prepare it so that you can either eat it on the spot, or take it with you for a picnic along the Han River. Located south of the Han, not far from Yeouido, at Noryangjin station on line 1. www.susansijang.co.kr (Korean).

2. **Gwangjang Market.** The go-to place for fabric in Korea; Gwangjang also carries an extensive selection of *hanbok* (Korean traditional clothing). A visual treat, even if you don't buy anything. Located in central Seoul near Cheonggyecheon Stream in Jongno and accessible by Jongno 5-ga station, line 1, exit 8, and Euljiro 4-ga station, lines 2 and 5. www.kwangjangmarket.co.kr (Korean).

3. **Seoul Folk Flea Market.** This market was established when the restoration of Cheonggyecheon Stream displaced a large number of small merchants from the Dokkaebi Market in Hwanghak-dong. The market is a good place to look for antiques, crafts, collectibles and souvenirs. Open from 10 a.m. to seven p.m. Near Cheonggyecheon Stream and Sinseoldong station, lines 1 and 2. www.seoulfolkfleamarket.com.

4. **Hongdae Park Market.** Held every weekend from March to November in Hongdae Park, the market features arts and crafts made by young local artists. It's a laid-back funky scene, and a great place to purchase a unique piece of art or pick up an accessory. Hongik University station, line 2.

5. **Yangjae Flower Market.** Located in southern Seoul, Yangjae contains over 100 flower shops, a large green house and an auction hall. It is particularly popular in spring and serves both retail and wholesale customers. Many visit just to look at—and smell—the merchandise. In addition to flowers Yangjae also features herbs, potted plants and shrubs. Yangjae station, line 3, exit 7 and then transfer to a Seongnam/Gwacheon bound bus or take a short cab ride.

DONGDAEMUN MARKET

Dongdaemun is a small, densely packed city unto itself. It contains some 30 shopping centers and roughly 30,000 stores in a ten-block area. Located near Dongdaemun (East Gate) and Dongdaemun station, the market complex is open all night and hums with activity well into the wee hours.

Hanok

Traditional Korean houses are known as *hanok* and are characterized by sloping, gently curved tiled roofs. Because of war-time destruction followed by rapid post-war growth, little of such classic housing remains in Seoul.

Bukchon Hanok Village lies on the slopes of Bugaksan Mountain and comprises over 800 traditional houses. The area is flanked by Gyeongbokgung Palace on one side and Changdeokgung on the other; Insadong lies to the south. At one time Bukchon was home to Joseon royalty and other big wigs, but in the 1930s population pressure and the decline of the Korean aristocracy caused these dwellings to be converted to use by commoners.

Bukchon is composed of winding hillside alleys of small homes; the attraction is not any one particular dwelling, but the totality of the village. For those overwhelmed by contemporary Seoul, Bukchon provides a window onto a less frenzied past.

A good place to start a visit is near Bukchon's entrance at the Bukchon Traditional Culture Center. The building is an example of *hanok* itself, and houses a museum and information center. Other attractions in the area include the Museum of Korean Buddhist Art, Gahoe Museum (which features folk paintings, amulets and other crafts) and Gahoe-dong #31, home to what is considered Bukchon's most picturesque alley. While some of the *hanok* have been converted into commercial establishments and restaurants, and others are museums and cultural properties, a large percentage of the *hanok* are actual homes. The best strategy for touring

Dongdaemun merchants sell everything from stationery to pets to sporting goods, but the market is world famous for its clothing, and is home to literally thousands of fashion designers and retailers. A garment can go from the planning to the production stage in a matter of hours, a time frame not lost on wholesalers from around Korea, and around the world

Dongdaemun's stores are divided into various buildings, and gen-

Bukchon is simply to wander about the alleys taking in the views.

Namsangol Hanok Village, a slice of ancient times in the heart of the city, is Seoul's other prime spot for appreciating *hanok's* enduring beauty. Located at the base of Namsan Mountain's north side, Namsangol is a folk village displaying the splendor of Joseon traditional architecture. Namsangol is composed of five traditional buildings, gardens and courtyards that were originally located at different sites around Seoul before being moved to form the village.

In addition to elegant buildings, Namsangol offers music and dance performances, as well as traditional wedding ceremonies and demonstrations of traditional games. Unlike Bukchon, Namsangol features several expansive houses which belonged to the upper classes and incorporated such elements as separate male and female living quarters. Moreover, the large courtyards of the aristocratic residences have been reproduced, and are ideal for strolling and contemplating the elegant design of the surrounding houses.

Namsangol is about the past, but also the future. In 1994, a time capsule representing 600 years of Seoul's history was buried on the site. The capsule is to be opened in 2394 to celebrate Seoul's 1000th year.

Popular with both locals and visitors, Namsangol is free and offers guided tours in English.

TAKE 5 FIVE UNUSUAL SEOUL MUSEUMS

Seoul is home to over 100 museums. Some, like the National Museum of Korea, require a whole day to properly explore, but there are others that are perfect for a quick visit if you are in the area.

1. **Lock Museum**. Not just any old locks, these are traditional and antique locks, keys, keyholders and furniture with locks. These unique pieces of art, culture and engineering have now disappeared in our era of mass production. The contemporary rust-colored building housing the museum is a Daehangno district landmark. www.lockmuseum.org.

2. **Owl Art & Craft Museum**. The name says it all. The museum is located in a small house, and specializes in owl objects (over 2,000 of them). Located in Samcheong-dong in central Seoul, the museum is open Thursday to Sunday. From Anguk station, line 3, take exit 2 on Samcheong-dong Road past the Korea Banking Institute. www.owlmuseum.co.kr (Korean).

3. **Seoul Museum of Chicken Art**. Two floors of chicken-themed objects from around the world. The pieces range from ancient relics to contemporary sculptures and paintings. Closed Mondays and holidays. Like the Owl Art & Craft Museum, it is a several-minute walk from Anguk station, line 3, exit 2. www.kokodac.com (Korean).

4. **Mokin Museum and Gallery**. *Mokin* are wooden dolls, and the museum has over 3,000 of them. Many of the small wooden people and animals are from Joseon times, and were buried with corpses to ward off evil spirits and ensure peace in the afterlife. The three-story building off the main street in Insadong has several galleries as well as a rooftop garden. Anguk station, line 3, exit 6 to the main street; the museum is near the Insadong information center. www.mokinmuseum.com (Korean).

5. **Teddy Bear Museum**. Want a novel way to learn about Korean history? Try the Teddy Bear Museum, located at Namsan's N Seoul Tower. The bears are dressed in traditional garb and teach visitors young and old about Seoul's past. There are also miniatures of various Seoul attractions, in case you can't make it to the real ones. Admission to the museum can be purchased as part of a package with other N Seoul Tower attractions, or by itself. Open daily 10 a.m. to 10 p.m.

They said it

"The difference between Seoul both north and south of the Han River is almost great enough to define two separate cities, both in appearance and atmosphere; the people who live and work in these two areas tend towards difference as well."

– Michael Hurt, commenting on the divergence between "new" Seoul south of the Han River, and "old" Seoul north of the river. The south is known for consumption, commerce and innovation, while the north has more established cultural and governmental institutions, and a greater number of historic structures and neighborhoods. Taken from "Seoul Streets: Part I," in the 2007 book *Korea Up Close: Photographic Encounters by Foreign Observers.*

erally grouped by type. They run the gamut from chic department store-like operations blasting trendy music, to tiny almost improvised stalls. Much of Dongdaemun is aimed at the wholesale trade, but the market has become increasingly popular with retail shoppers, who can get some great deals if they are willing to bargain and are not expecting changing rooms, sales staff and other amenities. Not everyone speaks English, but a merchant will put a number on a calculator and a shopper can then similarly counter offer.

To get in touch with youth fashion culture without spending hours traipsing from building to building and store to store, try the Dongdaemun Migliore Mall and the eight-floor 600-shop Doota Fashion Mall (in the Doosan Tower). These two complexes are visually exciting and fun, and don't be shocked to see the clothes on display pop up in department stores a short time later.

On the horizon is Dongdaemun Design Plaza (DDP), an exhibition and convention hall with design and media labs, a museum and an underground cultural plaza. The DDP and adjacent Dongdaemun Design Park, which will highlight cultural properties and provide green space, will open at the end of 2011.

They said it

DISTRICTS IN SEOUL
NORTH OF THE HAN RIVER
Jeongdong

Elegant Jeongdong is rich in cultural attractions and easy to explore. Located downtown near City Hall and Deoksugung Palace, it was known as Legation Street during the late nineteenth century because of the many foreign legations (diplomatic offices) and Westerners living in the area.

Jeongdong is a popular place to stroll and a favorite with young lovers. Love birds, however, should be careful; some believe that if a couple walks from the main street (Doldam-gil or Stonewall Road) alongside Deoksugung Palace into the Jeongdong area, they will break-up. Until about 20 years ago, Seoul's family court was located in this area, and angry couples would walk in together, but leave as divorced individuals. The easiest gateway to the area is City Hall station.

Itaewon

Itaewon has long been one of the most popular districts in Seoul with visitors and expats. It once had a seamy reputation as the place where local U.S. Army soldiers let off steam, but today has evolved into a more sophisticated, international destination.

Itaewon's main street is filled with shops selling antiques, knick-knacks, jewelry and clothing. Most merchants speak English and Japanese, and bargaining is common. If, for some reason, you need a New York Yankees cap or Green Bay Packers jacket while in Korea, you will find plenty to choose from in Itaewon. And if you can't find something off-the-rack, the district is known for its many tailors crafting made-to-order suits.

In the last several years Itawon has come into its own as a night life spot. There are still vintage expat bars showing NFL games on big screens, but there are also pubs, lounges, dance clubs and various

TAKE5 FIVE TALLEST BUILDINGS
IN SEOUL

Seoul is famous for its high-rises. It's not the height of any one building that is notable, but rather the incredible number of tall buildings, particularly apartment blocks. This list is subject to change -- on the horizon are a handful of super skyscrapers which will rank among the world's tallest buildings, and dwarf Seoul's current crop of biggies.

1. **Tower Palace 3 (Tower G).** Built in 2004, Tower Palace 3 is primarily an apartment building and is 73 stories high. It is the tallest building in Korea and stands 264 meters (866 feet) tall. By way of comparison, the Empire State Building measures 373 meters (1,224 feet), not including the antenna.

2. **Mok-dong Hyperion 1 (Tower A).** Built in 2003, Tower A is a residential building with 69 floors. It stands 256 meters (840 feet) tall.

3. **63 City.** One of Seoul's most famous buildings, the "63 Building" was constructed in 1985 and is 249 meters (817 feet) tall. At one time it was the tallest building in Asia. The building's 63 name is perhaps misleading; there are 60 stories above ground and three basement levels. In addition to offices, 63 houses over 90 stores, an IMAX theater, an aquarium with over 20,000 fish, a wedding hall and a convention center.

4. **Mok-dong Hyperion 1 (Tower B).** Built in 2003, Tower B is a sibling to Tower A, has 63 stories and measures 239 meters (784 feet). It is primarily an apartment building.

5. **Tower Palace 1 (Tower B).** Built in 2002, Tower B has 66 stories and stands 234 meters (768 feet) tall. Like Tower Palace 3 (Tower G) it is mostly residential.

quirky establishments.

Itaewon is also one of Seoul's most cosmopolitan areas, and features many foreign restaurants including Thai, Indian, Turkish, Mexican, French and Italian eateries. Itaewon is also home to the first permanent mosque in Korea, which opened in 1976.

There is an Itaewon stop on line 6 of the Seoul subway, and major hotels often provide shuttles to the area.

Camp Yongsan

Yongsan Garrison (Yongsan means "Dragon Mountain") is located in central Seoul near Itaewon, and is the headquarters for U.S. military personnel stationed in Korea. The base is home to roughly 17,000 U.S. Army soldiers, Department of Defense civilians and family members, and has the amenities, and feel, of a U.S. town. It possesses schools (elementary to university level), restaurants, shopping complexes, sports facilities, a hospital and a library.

Daehangno

Daehangno is a lively district popular for its arts and culture scene. Daehangno means "University Street," and it got this name because it used to be the home of Seoul National University prior to SNU's move in the mid-1970s.

Quaint cafes and restaurants line Daehangno's streets, and the

Did you know...

that the Yongsan Electronics Market has over 3,000 stores in more than a dozen buildings? The go-to place for everything from televisions to computers to hand-held devices and appliances, Yongsan attracts both wholesale and retail shoppers. Located near Yongsan station, line 1, the market is popular with bargain shoppers and techies wishing to ogle the latest in electronic and computer gadgets.

district is famous for its numerous theaters. A booth near Marronnier Park (Marronnier is French for "chestnut") has a listing of daily performances, and the staff can help with tickets and directions. Among the cultural draws in Daehangno are Samtoh's Blue Bird Theater, the Daehangno Arts Theater, Dongsoong Art Center and the Korean Culture and Arts Foundation. If you are on a tight budget, or pressed for time, Marronnier Park, especially on weekends, is a great place for free entertainment. There are street performances by young comedians, as well as occasional bands, artists, and singers. Hyehwa station on line 4 is the gateway to the area.

TAKE 5 FIVE LIVING NATURAL MONUMENTS IN SEOUL

South Korea has designated 387 Natural Monuments, 12 of which are in Seoul.

1. **Oriental oak (Natural Monument No. 271) in Sillim-dong.** Believed to be 1,000 years old, this is the oldest known tree in Seoul, and the only Seoul natural monument located south of the Han River.

2. **700-year-old juniper tree (No. 194) in Changdeokgung Palace.** This tree is famous for its unique, twisted appearance.

3. **Lacebark pine (No. 8) at the Constitutional Court.** This pine has been standing for about 600 years, and has become a symbol of hope and Korea's future. Some claim that the tree stopped growing during the Japanese occupation, and only regained its health after Korea's liberation in 1945. The tree is currently thriving.

4. **600-year old tara vine (No. 251) at Changdeokgung Palace.** The shape of this popular attraction resembles a dragon waiting for the rain. In ancient times, some believed that a dragon living beneath Seoul controlled the rain.

5. **500-year-old gingko tree (No. 59) in front of the Chinese shrine at Sungkyunkwan University.** Gingko trees are often used as symbols of Confucianism; this gingko was planted in 1519.

TAKE 5
BROTHER ANTHONY'S TOP FIVE
TEA HOUSES

Brother Anthony of Taizé was born in Cornwall, England in 1942 and is Emeritus Professor of English at Sogang University. He joined the French ecclesiastical monastic community of Taizé in 1969, and came to Korea in 1980. He has written many books and articles about medieval and early modern English literature, and is also recognized as a leading translator of Korean literature. Brother Anthony became a naturalized Korean citizen in 1994, and has been awarded the Ok-gwan (jade crown) Order of Merit for Culture by the Korean government. Visit his website at: hompi.sogang.ac.kr/anthony.

1. **Gwicheon**귀천. The name means "Back to Heaven," and it is the title of the most famous poem by the poet Cheon Sang- byeong (1930–1993). His wife Mok Sun-ok, opened the café in 1985 and still runs it. She is a very special person and a survivor of the Hiroshima bomb. Located in the southern half of the main Insadong street, the café is opposite the "Hae Jeong Hospital" sign, on the ground floor of a large gallery/café complex, away from the road. The mostly fruit teas are entirely homemade, with 모과차 (quince) and 유자차 (citron) highly celebrated. They are unlike teas with the same name served elsewhere, having matured for two to three years underground. The green tea is hand-dried in small quantities and not available elsewhere in Seoul. Tel: 02 734-2828 or 3210-2288. Jongno-gu Gwanhun-dong 83(서울시 종로구 관훈동). You can see the store from the Sudo-yakbang alley (수도약방). Anguk station, line 3, exit.

2. **Dagyeonghyangsil** 다경향실. The best place I know in Seoul for a selection of really fine leaf teas from Korea and China. In addition to green and "yellow" (oxidized) teas from Korea, as well as Chinese green, oolong and pu'er teas, it also serves traditional Korean fruit teas and a small selection of rice cakes and tea-sweets. Tel: 02 723-3651. Jongno-gu Gwanhun-dong 18 (Insadong, around Insa Art Plaza, on the right when walking from Jongno).

3. **Jidaebang** 지대방. The interior of this café has not changed in over 15 years. It might seem shabby to some, but others love it, as I

do. It serves traditional Korean teas, including green tea produced by its owner in Jirisan, a mountain in southern Korea. Among the more unusual and delicious teas are 모두다차 or *modudacha* ("everything possible tea"), a delicate concoction of some 40 different mountain herbs, and 솔바람차 ("pine-breeze tea"), a slightly effervescent infusion of pine needles. Tel: 02 738-5379. Around the center of the main Insadong street, on the left side, when walking from Jongno.

4. **Sanjungdawon** 산중다원. Most of Korea's great Buddhist temples have built tea houses for visitors, and some of them are truly palatial. However, visitors to 조계사 (Jogyesa), the temple in the center of Seoul one block west of Insadong, often have great difficulty finding its very un-palatial tea-room. It is concealed in a basement beneath the pavilion holding the great bell and drum, just in front of the main hall. It can be found by descending the stairs in front of the bell pavilion, plunging boldly into the corridor with the toilets, and making a sharp left as the corridor narrows. Shoes are removed upon entry, and guests sit on cushions on the carpeted floor. It is all very simple and temple-like, and features Korean green teas, traditional fruit and medicinal teas, and juices. Tel: 02 736-1678. 45 Gyeonji-dong Jongno-gu. Jonggak station, line 1, exit 2, walk about 70 meters (230 feet) and cross the stree,t then walk straight another100 meters (330 feet). The temple is on the left.

5. **Suyeonsanbang** 수연산방. This is a visually delightful tea room in a traditional Korean house. Yi Tae-jun, a novelist and Korean short story pioneer, had the place built to his design in 1933. He lived there until 1946 when he chose the North Korean side, as did many writers and intellectuals of the time. Members of his family still own the house, which is virtually unchanged from years ago, and serves traditional Korean teas and light snacks. Tel: 02 764-1736. 248 Seongbuk-dong Seongbuk-gu. Hanseongdae-ipgu station, line 4, exit 6. From there, take bus 1111 or 2112, or Maeul bus 3 and get off at Dongbang Daehakwon. It is right behind Geumwang-donkkas restaurant (금왕돈까스) which has a big yellow sign.

Insadong

Once known by foreigners as "Mary's Alley," Insadong is a cultural district in the heart of the city. It should rank high on any Seoul "must" list.

Insadong's streets and alleys are lined with art galleries and stores filled with antiques and Korean crafts. Traditional Korean paper (known as *hanji* and made from Mulberry bark) is particularly popular, as are fans, masks, celadon pottery and lacquered items. Prices range from pocket change for Korea-themed knick-knacks, to the very expensive for select antiques.

The traditionally designed Kyung-in Museum of Fine Art (www. kyunginart.co.kr) features a tea house and exhibition spaces and is an elegant and rewarding attraction. Another popular spot is Ssamziegil, a multi-story building with a rooftop restaurant and dozens of unique shops.

Insadong is a great area for tea houses as well as restaurants specializing in traditional cuisine. Sunday is a particularly good day to visit as the principal artery is closed to traffic and there are street performances, including a reenactment of a Joseon-era police patrol at 5 p.m. Visitors should take the time to meander through the alleys and lanes that lie off Insadong's major street. The alleys and lanes provide you with a sense of what old Seoul must have been like centuries ago. Anguk station on line 3 provides the easiest access to the area, and visitors can orient themselves with a visit to the Bukinsa Tourist Information Center. Other nearby subway stations include Jonggak and Jongno 3-ga.

Jongno and Pimatgol

Jongno, located next to Insadong, is known for its private language academies (*hakwon*), music stores, and nightlife.

Tapgol or Pagoda Park is Seoul's oldest western-style park and it lies in the center of the district. The park, which features a 10-tier pagoda, holds special significance to Seoulites. It was here, as well as at many locations across Korea, that the March 1, 1919 declaration against Japanese rule was proclaimed. This March 1 (known locally as *Samil Undong*) protest is commemorated by murals in the park depicting the

Korean struggle for freedom. Tapgol is a great spot for people-watching, and a nice escape from the bustle of downtown. Some of Seoul's seniors congregate here to play checkers and other games.

Pimatgol is not a district *per se*, but rather a small historic area that has been disappearing as the area is redeveloped. In Joseon times, Pimatgol was a long alley that ran the length of the main street in Jongno. Literally meaning "path to avoid horses," it was used

TAKE 5 FIVE PLACES TO WITNESS
THE CHANGING SEASONS

It goes without saying that centrally-located, tree-covered Namsan Mountain is an ideal location to observe the season's changing colors, but there are others.

1. **Yeouido Park.** With over 1,400 cherry trees, Yeouido Park is without question one of the best places to welcome spring. Falling cherry blossoms cover the paths and walkways of the park, and its location on Yeouido Island makes it ideal for a family outing.

2. **Kyung Hee University.** The campus in Dongdaemun-gu near Hoegi station in northeastern Seoul is popular with young couples who stroll amongst the cherry trees. Other bucolic university campuses in Seoul include those of Korea University and Ewha Woman's University.

3. **Changdeokgung Palace.** In one palace garden alone there are over 100 types of trees, ideal for viewing the fall foliage. Easiest access is Anguk station on line 3, or Hyehwa station, line 4.

4. **Jeong-dong.** A popular spot in autumn, centrally located Jeong-dong is popular with couples. During the late Joseon period, Jeong-dong was one of Seoul's foreigner enclaves. Many of the historic buildings remain, and combined with the brilliance of the autumn leaves, make for a romantic stroll. This area is in the vicinity of Deoksugung and Gyeonghuigung Palaces. Seodaemun station, line 5.

5. **Hongneung Arboretum.** This enchanting sanctuary was founded in 1922 and has nine gardens with about 2,000 types of trees and 65 species of wildlife, most of them birds. Closest subway is Korea University station, line 6.

by commoners wishing to avoid the main street, where they might encounter Korean nobility riding on horseback. In that era, commoners were expected to prostrate themselves until the nobility had passed, at which time they could again stand up. Pimatgol would become a popular area for common people to eat and drink, and is still a favored district among locals.

Myeong-dong

Centrally-located Myeong-dong is a trendy shopping area home to countless department, outlet and specialty stores. Among the best known establishments are the Lotte and Shinsegae department stores, and the Migliore and Avatar shopping malls. In the early evening, Myeong-dong's streets are thronged with young people shopping for clothes and cosmetics, eating ice cream and other treats, and showing off their latest purchases.

Myeong-dong is famous for its cathedral which was constructed in the 1890s. It went on to play an important role in South Korea's democracy movement, and served as a haven for protestors and dissidents.

Myeong-dong also serves as a banking center, and institutions including UNESCO and the Chinese Embassy are in the district. At mid-day, armies of white-shirted office workers in search of lunch emerge from their cubicles and pack the district. Myeongdong station on line 4 is an easy gateway to an area which sees about two million visitors daily.

Hongdae University Area

Hongdae, Sinchon and Edae are adjacent districts that form a university mega-area in Mapo-gu in western Seoul. Yonsei, Ewha, Sogang and Hongik universities are all in the vicinity, rendering the district a student mecca whose vibrant shops, clubs, bars and restaurants keep it humming at all hours. The large population of international students makes it a diverse area, and the clubs in Hongdae are particularly popular with young foreigners. This is the go-to area to catch up-and-coming Korean bands. Hongdae is well served by several subway stations.

TAKE 5 FIVE HIGHEST MOUNTAINS SURROUNDING SEOUL

1 **Bukhansan** (836.5 meters; 2,744 feet).
2. **Dobongsan** (739.5 meters; 2,426 feet).
3. **Suraksan** (638 meters; 2,093 feet).
4. **Gwanaksan** (629 meters; 2,064).
5. **Cheonggyesan** (618 meters; 2,028 feet).

Yeouido

Yeouido, sometimes called the "Manhattan of Seoul," is an island in the Han River. It is notable for the 63 City building, the Korea Stock Exchange, Yeouido Park and the Republic of Korea's National Assembly building. Yeouido is actually not much of an island as it is barely separated from the Han's southern bank.

Skyscrapers dot the Seoul skyline, but nowhere is this more evident than in Yeouido. The area serves as the headquarters for insurance, broadcast and finance companies. For visitors, the 63 City building with its basement aquarium and observatory is a big draw. The views from what was until recently Seoul's tallest building are particularly spectacular at night. Another attraction is the Yeouido Full Gospel Church, which draws tens of thousands of worshippers every Sunday.

Yeouido is an excellent gateway from which to explore the Han River, and there are boat cruises arriving at and departing from the Yeouido Ferry Terminal. The Yeouinaru and Yeouido stations on line 5 provide access to Yeouido Island.

DISTRICTS SOUTH OF THE RIVER

Gangnam

"Gangnam" means "south of the river," and this large area became populous and wealthy during the boom of the 1970s and 1980s. It is known for its shopping and nightlife, as well as for its expensive apartments, high quality schools and many private educational academies or *hakwons*. It is also the home of the massive COEX mall and accompanying convention center, trade center and hotels. Just to the north of COEX is Bongeunsa, a Buddhist temple dating to CE 794 which is open to visitors. Gangnam station on line 2 is one of the busiest in the Seoul subway system, and exit 7 leads to the main drag, which is packed with restaurants and bars.

Apgujeong

Apgujeong is a "*dong*" in the larger "*gu*" of Gangnam. High-end restaurants and stores line Apgujeong's streets, and it is one of Seoul's trendiest areas. Famous artists, photographers and designers have their studios in Apgujeong. The hip and the chic either live in the area or visit to shop and hobnob. Rodeo Street in particular is famous as the launching pad for South Korean fashion and other trends. In addition to the glittery Galleria Department Store, Rodeo features dozens of clothing stores, boutiques and galleries. To see South Korean youth culture in full bloom, get off Rodeo and explore some of the area's side streets.

Sometimes, in order to be a member of the glitterati you need more than nice clothes. Part of the entry fee may be cosmetic surgery, and Apgujeong is the leading place for such procedures in South Korea. Many people come to Seoul to visit one of Apgujeong's top-flight clinics, and then enjoy a little post-op R & R. Apgujeong station on line 3 is the gateway to the area.

Did you know. . .

that Seoul has its own French enclave, known as Seorae Village? The village is home to hundreds of French expats and sprung up in the mid-1980s when Seoul's French school relocated to the area. Located in Banpo-dong near the Express Bus Terminal station in southern Seoul, Seorae is, not surprisingly, a great place for wine, cheese and French bread. A few of the street signs are even in French, and some of the sidewalk bricks are painted with the famous *tricolore* red, white and blue of the French flag. Visitors can also enjoy the hilltop park known as Montmartre.

Cheongdam

Cheongdam-dong is a red-hot shopping and restaurant district to the east of Apgujeong-dong. Like its neighbor to the west, Cheongdam is a top spot for boutiques, galleries, cosmetic surgery clinics and exclusive restaurants. Cheongdam cultivates a more sophisticated and less showy

A River Runs Through It

London has the Thames, Paris the Seine and Seoul the Han. The 514 kilometer-long (320 mile) Han River is the second longest river in South Korea, trailing only the Nakdong River. The Han is considered the heart of Seoul, and divides the city into northern and southern halves.

The river has played a crucial role in Seoul's economic development and history. It once served as the primary means of transportation from the West Sea port city of Incheon to Seoul, and was frequented by large junks and small river steamboats. The Han also provided a southern defense when Seoul was confined to the area north of the river.

Until fairly recently, business, shopping and entertainment were generally confined to the area north of the river, while the southern part was chiefly residential. This changed in the 1980s, and some of the most popular shopping and entertainment zones in Seoul, as well as many corporate office towers, are now located south of the Han.

The 1988 Olympics were the crowning achievement of the "Miracle on the Han," and the river's once barren banks were planted with trees and grass. The river and surrounding area remain a work in progress, and the Han is a centerpiece in efforts to improve Seoul environmentally and recreationally. Already, the Han River parks stretch from one end of the city to the other, and provide Seoulites with venues for outdoor activities of all types. On the water itself, windsurfing, waterskiing, and sailing have become popular, and fishing retains its timeless allure. Tour boats and ferries also travel up and down the river, and nighttime cruises are particularly popular.

During the summer, more than 150,000 people visit the banks of the river each day, and there are dozens of kilometers of paths for cycling, jogging, and inline skating. The Han is also popular for picnics and dates, and is a venue for amateur musicians who, in certain locations, will belt out a tune for passers-by.

TAKE 5 FIVE FREE (OR INEXPENSIVE)
THINGS TO DO ALONG THE HAN RIVER

1. **Banpo Bridge Water Show**. Banpo Bridge has been outfitted with 380 nozzles that send plumes of water cascading into the river 20 meters (65 feet) below. After dark, the jets of water are illuminated with colored lights, making for a spectacular nighttime show. Banpo is the world's longest fountain bridge and spouts 190 tons of water per minute.

2. **Bike Riding**. The Han River has 97 kilometers (60 miles) of paths along its banks dedicated for cycling, jogging and skating. Bicycles can be rented for about 3,000 won ($2.70) an hour, and provide not only exercise but also an excellent and safe way to sightsee along the river.

3. **Picnics**. With wide open spaces of grass and refreshing cool breezes, it is no wonder that the Han is an oasis for Seoulites seeking to beat the summer heat. Stores located along the river sell snacks, chicken, and even beer. In the evenings, amateur musicians provide impromptu concerts on the north bank near the Seongsan Bridge.

4. **Special Events and Festivals**. In the summer, Korean comedy programs are often filmed at various locations along the river. In October, the Han River High Wire World Championship is held during the day, and in the evening the Seoul Fireworks Festival lights up the sky with spectacular displays.

5. **An Evening Cruise.** A number of large pleasure boats ply the Han during the warmer months. There are several courses to choose from, and each cruise lasts from 60 to 90 minutes. For the adventuresome, there is even a pirate boat! Prices vary depending on the length of the cruise and number of stops. Tickets are 8,000-16,000 won each (about $6 to $14).

6. **Fishing**. The Han is a popular place for fishing, and a license is not required. Most Han River fishermen release their catch, unless the fish in question are *bung-eo, ing-eo* (both species of carp) or *jangeo* (eel). The *jangeo* are often eaten, and according to more than a few "wise" old fishermen, are good for male stamina. The *bungeo* and *ingeo* are usually made into medicine -- the *ingeo* is said to aid in fertility, while *bungeo* is good for general well-being, particularly in the elderly.

image than Apgujeong, and is ever so slightly off the beaten track. In the last several years, international brands like Hermes have been setting up stores around Dosan Park. The park, which is named after Korean patriot Dosan Ahn Chang-ho, is a peaceful green spot where one can take time out from shopping or munching.

Jamsil

Jamsil is best known for its role in hosting the 1988 Olympics. The district is in Songpa-gu, which lies to the east of Gangnam-gu. Olympic Park and Olympic Stadium are still very much in use here. Jamsil is also home to Lotte World, which is the world's largest indoor amusement park.

GREEN SPACES

Seoul's green spaces come in many forms: elegant palace gardens, mountain areas, and university campuses as well as parks, squares, and preservation and recreation areas. Each of the following are big enough that one could spend an entire day exploring.

Olympic Park

The expansive Olympic Park is a huge oasis of green and tranquility in the midst of one of the world's most bustling cities. It commemorates the 1988 Olympics and is located in southeastern Seoul, south of the Han. (Olympic Park is separate from Olympic Stadium, which lies several kilometers to the west).

Olympic Park is home to more than 200 outdoor sculptures, as well as the spectacular World Peace Gate which stands 24 meters (80 feet) tall and 62 meters (200 feet) long. The bowed, wing-like top pieces

Did you know. . .

that there are 24 bridges spanning the Han River in Seoul? The first permanent bridge was the Hangang Railroad Bridge, which opened in 1900. In Joseon times, in order for the king to cross the Han, 70 large boats were tethered and large planks placed between them to create a floating bridge.

They said it

are adorned with colorful and traditional designs, and the structure is playful yet powerful and inspiring.

Olympic Park comprises the 2.7 kilometer (1.7 mile) Baekje Kingdom Mongchontoseong Fortress, as well as the Olympic Museum, the SOMA Museum of Art, the Olympic Indoor Swimming Pool and many walking and bike trails. Mongchontoseong station on line 8 and Olympic Park station on line 5 are the closest subway stops

Seoul Grand Park

A wonderful place to relax and stroll, Seoul Grand Park features trees and trails, a botanical garden and a lake. It's a great place for kids, and is home to a major zoo as well as Seoul Land amusement park. Once you've finished your ice cream and wiped your hands, you can also visit the substantial National Museum of Contemporary Art. Seoul Grand Park is in the eastern part of the city, north of the Han River, and accessible by Seoul Grand Park station on line 4.

Seoul Forest

Seoul Forest was at one time a royal hunting ground. It later became Ttukseom Sports Park and had a horse racing track, but has now been returned to nature. Seoul Forest is bordered on its south side by the Han River and on the west by a tributary of the Han. It is modeled on such urban havens as New York's Central Park, and features over 100,000 trees and 100 different animal species. The Park's five themed areas provide plenty to explore, and Seoul Forest is an excellent place to walk, bicycle or Rollerblade (rentals are available). Ttukseom station on line 2 is the place to kick off a Forest visit.

Seonyudo Park

Seonyudo is an island in the Han River featuring an environmentally themed park with an aquatic botanical garden, a museum and a pavilion modeled on traditional housing. The arch-shaped Seonyu bridge, also known as Rainbow Bridge, links the park with the Yangwha Area south of the Han.

Seonyudo, which is on the site of a former water purification plant, has exceptional views and is a wonderful spot to picnic or enjoy a meal from the on-site cafeteria. Easiest access is probably via a short cab ride from Mangwon station on line 6 on the north side of the Han.

Another island in the Han is Natural Habitat Park. This ecological preserve for migratory birds lies to the east of Seonyudo. Thousands of birds on their way to or from Siberia and Mongolia stop in the habitat, which is crossed by the Seogang Bridge. This island spot is limited to the feathered and winged (no people allowed).

World Cup Park

Surrounding World Cup Stadium and World Cup Mall in western Seoul are five connected parks, including a nine-hole golf course and many other athletic facilities. The site used to be Seoul's principal landfill—holding 92 million tons of garbage—until it was redeveloped for recreational use and ecological conservation.

Pyeonghwa Park, a popular spot for picnics, is nearest the stadium and features a pond, playground and small forest. The highest elevation in the area is found at Haneul Park, which is a grass covered mountain providing excellent views of Seoul and environs. Beneath the vegetation lies a giant garbage mound; but don't worry, it doesn't smell and you wouldn't know unless someone told you. The whole area comprises roughly 3.5 square kilometers (1.3 square miles). From the World Cup Stadium station, line 6, take exit 1, cross the street to Mapo Agriculture-Fisheries Market and catch the shuttle bus for the parks.

Food

Korean food calls on ancient traditions, but is also fresh, versatile and very twenty-first century. Recently, it has become the darling of foodies in Europe and North America. Spicy, briny, bold, and invigorating are all words used to describe Korean cuisine.

If you are new to Korean food, you are in for a real treat and will become a convert in short order.

Korean food gets its characteristic kick from the hot chilies, garlic, ginger, soy sauce and sesame commonly used in its preparation. It can be a labor intensive cuisine, and many of the side dishes are pickled and fermented.

True, Korean food is wonderfully tangy, savory and satisfying, but it does more than just taste good. Ask any local about a favorite dish, and you're bound to hear about how it promotes digestion, longevity and general well-being.

There's plenty to keep a gourmand busy — the bounty of the waters off the Korean Peninsula and the local harvest make for a healthy and well-balanced diet of fresh and fermented vegetables, whole grains, seafood and meat.

For those wishing to sample international cuisine, Seoul presents many options. Italian, French, Japanese, Chinese and North American food are popular, and there are also Thai, Indian and even Mexican

They said it

"There is perhaps no food more accessible, in any culture, than meat grilled over an open flame, and in Seoul you can't walk down a street, whether in the über-trendy Apgujeong neighborhood or a grayer district like Dongdaemun, without inhaling the invigorating fumes of charcoal fires."

— *New York Times* columnist Matt Gross writing in 2008.

restaurants. There's also fast food in the Land of Morning Calm. In addition to the fare offered by the global chains, local twists include donuts with green tea icing, corndogs sprouting crinkle fries and the ubiquitous spicy fried chicken. No matter what kind of food you like, you won't go hungry in Seoul.

Dining out in Korea is a social affair. The tables are large and the dishes abundant, as if begging diners to share. Many meals require audience participation, including grilling dishes at the table or tending to a bubbling hot pot.

Koreans love eating, and for good reason. Dig in!

A KOREAN FOOD PRIMER

RICE DISHES

Bap: **Rice.** The foundation of Korean meals, rice accompanies most dishes and is a base in many others. Sometimes white rice is mixed with brown rice, beans, millet or barley for added texture and nutritional value.

Bibimbap: **A bowl of rice topped with mixed vegetables and a fried egg.** Served with a spicy sauce and mixed together at the table. A standard Korean dish, *bibimbap* is simple, healthy and tasty.

Gimbap: **Rice and other ingredients rolled in seaweed.** Do not confuse *gimbap* with sushi. The two are not the same. Sure, they both contain seaweed and rice, and yes, like the *maki* roll, *gimbap* is rolled. But do not expect the sweet vinegary essence of sushi rice. *Gimbap* is more proletarian and affordable than sushi, and is often brought on outings since it is very portable.

SIDES AND SALADS

Cheongpo-muk: **Mung bean jelly and other ingredients.** Ideal for hot summer days, this salad sees mung bean jelly mixed with matchstick slices of meat, vegetables and shredded lettuce and served with a soy-based dressing. Mung bean jelly is similar to tofu in its block-like appearance and smooth texture.

Haepari-naengchae: **A cold salad that mixes shredded jellyfish, Asian pear and garlic in a mustard vinaigrette.** Usually served as part of a set meal, it's a tangy delight.

Namul: **Edible greens, herbs, leaves and roots.** These vegetable side dishes are typically blanched and seasoned. Popular *namul* include *chwi-namul* (wild asters), *kongnamul* (soybean sprouts), *gosari-namul* (bracken shoots) and *sigeumchi-namul* (spinach). *Namul* are generally served as side dishes, although some vegetarian and health conscious restaurants turn a sampler plate of these foraged treats into a main dish.

NOODLES

Guksu and *myeon*: **Noodles.** There are dozens of kinds of noodles and noodle dishes in Korea. The noodles themselves are typically made from buckwheat and regular wheat flour, although there are other varieties. Noodle shapes vary as well, and include thick hand-cut noodles and thin white *somyeon* style noodles. Stir fried noodle dishes are made from *ramyeon*, *udong*, and *dangmyeon* (a transparent sweet potato noodle).

Bibim-naengmyeon: **Cold wheat noodles with hot chili sauce.** Served with matchstick vegetables and other ingredients, this is a popular summer dish and delicious in its combination of icy and spicy.

***Japchae*: Seasoned transparent noodles.** The noodles are combined with sautéed vegetables including mushrooms, spinach, and carrot, and mixed with soy, sesame, and sugar sauce. *Japchae* is a great introduction to Korean cuisine for those wary of spicy food.

***Kalguksu*: Hand-cut flour noodles served in a clear chicken, beef, shellfish or dried anchovy stock.** Accented with mixed vegetables and sometimes clams.

TAKE5 FIVE KOREAN
FOOD CLASSICS

If you don't have time to try all of what Seoul's culinary scene has to offer, be sure to sample at least one or two of these standards.

1. ***Galbi-jjim***. Short ribs, along with mushrooms, chestnuts, ginko nuts and carrots are simmered in a complex broth of soy, green onion, garlic and pear juice until they tenderly fall off the bone.

2. ***Bulgogi***. Well-marbled cuts of meat, usually beef, are marinated in a sweet soy sauce, then grilled over an open flame or cooked at the table on a metal dish. Served with lettuce and *ssamjang* (spicy paste) for wrapping into neat bundles. Along with *galbi-jjim*, it provides a great introduction to Korean food.

3. ***Dolsot-bibimbap***. A bed of rice served in a hot stone bowl is blanketed by seasoned vegetables, a raw egg and usually some meat and kimchi. Soul-satisfying and filling.

4. ***Kimchi-jjigae***. A fiery pot of stew bubbling with kimchi and either pork or fish such as tuna or saury. Eaten with rice for a light dinner or lunch. It is tasty in summer and winter, and a killer for colds or jet lag. Novices may want to work their way up to this spicy dish.

5. ***Mul-naengmyeon***. Refreshing in summer and invigorating in winter, this dish's chewy noodles are served in a cold kimchi and beef broth garnished with sliced brisket, Asian pear, thin slices of radish and a hard-boiled egg.

Mulnaengmyeon: Cold noodles in soup with brisket, sliced pear and a hardboiled egg. Popular in summer.

Ramyeon. Instant noodles cooked with green onions and a fiery seasoning packet. Variations include *tteok-ramyeon* (noodles with sliced rice cakes), *mandu-ramyeon* (noodles with dumplings) and cheese-*ramyeon* (noodles topped with a slice of processed cheese). The latter sounds unappetizing, but the melted cheese moderates the heat of the broth.

SOUPS AND STEWS

Soup in Korea is known as "*guk*" or "*tang.*" Soup accompanies many meals in Korea, and ranges from humble seaweed soup to richer and more elaborate concoctions. Soups are generally of three types: clear broth seasoned with soy sauce or salt, thicker soups seasoned with fermented soybean paste, and beef or pork stock soups. The Korean word for stew is *jjigae*.

Doenjang-jjigae: Fermented soybean paste stew served with tofu, mixed vegetables and sometimes clams.

Juk: Porridge. *Jatjuk* is one variety, and it consists of finely ground rice simmered over low heat until a thick porridge forms. Ground pine nuts are added to boost texture, taste and nutrition. Like oatmeal, *juk* is mellow in taste and is serious comfort food. Sometimes small bowls of *juk* are served as part of larger meals to stimulate the appetite.

Did you know. . .

that there is now a Zagat guide for Seoul? The Seoul edition debuted in 2010 and features reviews of 287 local restaurants by 4,000 Seoul diners. Some of the reviews appear in English on the Zagat website.

Kimchi-jjigae: Kimchi stew. Typically served in a bubbling earthenware pot, kimchi-*jjigae* features a spicy broth chock-full of its star ingredient.

Maeuntang: Fresh fish boiled with seasonal vegetables in a fiery broth. Shellfish is sometimes added.

Mandu-guk: Dumpling soup. Dumplings stuffed with tofu, meat, vegetables and/or kimchi are added to a beef or anchovy stock with egg, seaweed and green onions.

TAKE5 FIVE FOODS
FOR CELEBRATIONS

These culinary delights, consumed on strategic days of the year with hopes for good health and fortune, are also eaten year-round.

1. *Tteok-guk*. Traditionally served on the Lunar New Year, it is a clear broth dotted with sliced rice cakes, and garnished with ground meat, fried eggs cut into shapes and green onions. Perfect for a light lunch.
2. *Ogokbap*. Rice bowl comprised of five grains and typically eaten on Daeboreum, which celebrates the first full moon of the lunar year.
3. *Songpyeon*. Half-moon-shaped rice cakes stuffed with sweet fillings and steamed over a bed of pine needles. Typically served during Chuseok, the Korean Harvest Festival, as an ancestral offering.
4. *Patjuk*. Served during winter solstice, this red bean porridge is peppered with small, round rice cakes.
5. *Samgyetang*. Consumed during *sambok* (the three hottest days of the year). This dish consists of a whole chicken stuffed with rice, ginseng, jujubes and other ingredients, and served in a clear broth to provide stamina in the heat.

They said it

"For people who treat eating like it's an extreme sport, Korean food levels with the X-Games. There is much here to challenge your conventional concepts of food. This is a land where kids may turn down a slice of chocolate cake but ravenously rip apart a package of dried-buttered-cuttlefish. There are hot dog and donut vendors on the streets next to silkworm larvae (reminded me of overcooked shrimp)."

– Joe McPherson from "What do You Put in Your Mouth?" in the 2007 book *Korea Up Close Photographic Encounters by Foreign Observers*.

Miyeokguk: **Seaweed in a clear beef or anchovy based broth.** Often consumed for breakfast, it is high in calcium and a staple for women in the weeks following childbirth.

Sundubu-jjigae: **Tofu stew.** Soft tofu and chili flakes dominate a ground pork or shellfish stock. A freshly cracked egg is added to the bubbling pot for body, and chili peppers, enoki mushrooms, clams and green onions round out the mix. Served with the ubiquitous fire-retardant sticky rice.

Seolleong-tang: **A beef soup.** Features a hearty beef stock and slivered meat, *kkakdugi* (radish kimchi) and other vegetables.

COOKING METHODS
Stir Fried
Bokkeum. Most stir-fried dishes are seasoned with sesame oil, green onion, sesame seeds, salt and pepper. Kimchi-*bokkeumbap* features fried rice as a vehicle for kimchi, meat and vegetables; it is popular at home and in casual restaurants.

TAKE **5** ANDREW SALMON'S TOP FIVE
PLACES TO EAT IN SEOUL

Seoul-based reporter Andrew Salmon wrote restaurant reviews on behalf of *The Korea Herald* and The JoongAng Daily from 1997 to 2007. He is the author of the books *Seoul Food Finder* (2002), *American Business and the Korean Miracle: US Enterprises in Korea, 1866 - the Present* (2003) and *To the Last Round: The Epic British Stand on the Imjin River, Korea, 1951* (Aurum Press 2009). His website is www.tothelastround.wordpress.com.

1. **Doorei (Korean traditional food, Insa-dong).** Beautiful location inside a sensitively converted back-alley *hanok*. This high-end establishment offers a range of traditional Korean grub, and one of the best selections of traditional Korean booze. Equally popular with local politicians and well-heeled tourists.

2. **Chogatjib (Korean ribs, Mapo).** Mapo is Seoul's meat mecca, and this always-crowded, rough-and-ready joint is the most popular spot in the district. The superb pork galbi, homemade fermented bean paste sauce and iced water kimchi are worth the wait for seats.

3. **3 Alley Pub (Pub grub, Itaewon).** This Itaewon watering hole, popular with a 30-to 40-something crowd, is not as raucous as competing establishments, but offers Seoul's widest (and best) selection of beer taps. With so many "foreign" restaurants in Seoul offering dull and overpriced copies of hotel coffee shop cuisine, this is the place for stick-to-your-ribs international pub grub.

4. **Villa Sortino (Italian, Itaewon).** A brilliantly designed complex with a Milanese-style bar, a terrace-style dining room, and private dining in the wine cellar. Villa Sortino offers fine Italian food from Seoul's very own Sicilian son, Head Chef Santino Sortino. Pricey, but the perfect place for those occasions when a well-off acquaintance offers to take you out for dinner, or when you need to impress that key business contact or certain someone.

5. **Taco (Tex-Mex, Noksapyeong).** A cheap and cheerful spot opposite the Yongsan U.S. Army base that is run by a Korean who used to live in Mexico. The hearty tacos, burritos and enchiladas are as good as any you will find in Seoul, and cheaper than most.

Broiled or Grilled

Gui. Many grilled dishes are marinated in a mixture of soy sauce, sugar, sesame oil, green onions, garlic, and sometimes red pepper. Many fish dishes, however, are grilled with a simple dash of salt. A seafood favorite is *jangeo-gui*, which is eel glazed with a mixture of soy sauce, sugar, sesame oil and salt and then grilled. It's said to have stamina-increasing properties.

Dumplings

Mandu. Thin rounds of dough are wrapped around fillings that include tofu, meat, vegetables, and kimchi. These are steamed (*jjin-mandu*), boiled (*mul-mandu*) or fried (*gun-mandu*).

Hot Pot

Jeongol. Korean hot pots are generally cooked at the table, offering a little tableside drama. The *dubu-jeongol*, or tofu hotpot, is a delicious collision of sliced tofu, ground beef, bamboo shoots, green onions and more.

Simmered/Braised/Fried

Jjim, jorim: **Seasoned meat, fish and vegetables are steamed or braised until fork tender.**

Dubu-jorim: **Bite sized squares or domino planks of tofu.** First fried, then simmered in soy sauce, the tofu is served as a side dish.

Jeon: **Pan-fried dishes including vegetables that have been dipped in flour then coated with egg.** Fried slices of summer squash are a common side dish.

Samgyeopsal: **Slices of pork belly kissed with a spicy sauce.** *Samgyeopsal* is grilled tableside and served with lettuce, rice, sliced garlic and *ssamjang* (a spicy paste) for packing into bundles. A great dish to share with friends.

FOOD SERVED RAW

Hoe: Raw fish served without rice. "Hoe" is the Korean word for what is called "sashimi" in Japan. In Korea, a platter of assorted sliced and prepared raw fish (which often includes halibut and skate) is known as *modumhoe*.

Hoe-deotbap: Rice topped with diced raw fish and matchstick raw vegetables. Veggies include carrot, radish sprouts, lettuce, and sliced gim (dried seaweed). Served with a seasoned chile sauce.

Yukhoe: Usually served at banquets or as part of a hotel meal, raw meat is prepared like tartar and seasoned with sesame oil, soy and sugar. Served with planks of Asian pear and crowned with a raw quail's egg yolk.

MIND YOUR MANNERS

Korean table etiquette is similar to that of Western countries. No elbows on the table, chew with your mouth closed and don't use your hands (in most cases) to pick up your food. If you are dining at a traditional restaurant where patrons sit on the floor at low tables, remove your shoes. The shoe rack at the entrance and the paper slippers on offer will tip you off.

Some other observances to keep you in your hosts' good graces are as follows: Use your spoon for rice, soups and stews; for everything else

Did you know...

that Seoul has a museum devoted to kimchi? The Pulmuone Kimchi Museum (www.kimchimuseum.or.kr) opened in 1986 and is located in the COEX mall. The museum provides a full exposition on the national dish, and features historical items as well as various displays and models. There is also the Tteok Museum (featuring rice cakes and traditional kitchenware) located at the Institute of Korean Traditional Food (www.kfr.or.kr) in Jongno-gu.

use chopsticks. Don't hold the rice or soup bowl in your hand as you eat. And never leave your chopsticks standing upright in a bowl of rice as this symbolizes the burning of incense at ancestral worship.

Finally, at the end of the meal, expect to do battle over the bill. Splitting the check in Korea is virtually unheard of, and the "host" typically pays. Good news, however, for those accustomed to leaving a 15 or 20 percent gratuity, tipping is not customary in Korea.

TAKE5 FIVE KINDS OF KIMCHI

Koreans proudly boast that there are over 200 types of kimchi. Rich with lactic acid bacteria, kimchi is one of the world's top health foods and Koreans eat an average of 35 kilos (77 pounds) yearly. Don't miss out, although rookies should probably take the spicy dish in moderation.

1. *Baechu*-kimchi. The classic Korean kimchi made with Napa cabbage. Whole cabbage heads are soaked in brine, and the leaves are then stuffed with a mixture of seafood, garlic, ginger, greens, onions, and more. Served at nearly every meal.

2. *Kkakdugi*-kimchi. Small crisp cubes of radish fermented with chili powder and garlic. After the abovementioned *baechu* kimchi, kkakdugi is one of the most common kinds of kimchi found at restaurants.

3. *Chonggak*-kimchi. Sometimes referred to as "bachelor kimchi," whole small radishes, including their green leafy tops, are fermented with garlic, ginger and chili powder.

4. *Nabak*-kimchi. A restorative water kimchi in which radishes are cut into slender rectangles and accompanied by green onion floating in a slightly sour brine. It has just enough heat to wake up the taste buds.

5. *Oisobagi*. Cucumbers are split and soaked in brine, then filled with a mixture of ginger, garlic, chili and various ingredients. A cool summertime treat, and an easy entry into the world of kimchi.

THE DOG ISSUE

It is illegal to eat dog meat in Korea, and a prohibition against the practice was introduced in the 1980s. Many Koreans are repelled by the practice, and local animal rights activists have campaigned to rid the country of the tradition. Conservative proponents of dog meat view such efforts as unnecessary meddling, and often give the debate a nationalist spin. Moreover, they maintain that the dogs in question are not—and never have been—pets, and so eating dog shouldn't be viewed as different from consuming beef or pork.

For the squeamish tourist, there is no reason for concern. You won't unwittingly be served dog, nor will you find it on a menu. Jokes about the matter are generally not appreciated.

TAKE5 FIVE KOREAN
SIDE DISHES

Banchan are the parade of side dishes that arrive at your table in a Korean restaurant. They are always an adventure in flavor and texture. There are many such dishes and they change often, but the following are commonly served. (Kimchi is standard and so is not included here).

1. *Gim*. Flat sheets of laver (a kind of seaweed) are brushed with sesame oil and sprinkled with salt, then roasted. Wrap it around small clumps of rice.
2. *Gamja-jorim*. Small potatoes or potato chunks are simmered in a sweet soy sauce.
3. *Kongjang*. Black beans are cooked, then seasoned with sugar and soy sauce and reduced until syrupy. Served garnished with sesame seeds.
4. *Maneul-jangajji*. Garlic is pickled in a sweet soy sauce with vinegar. Excellent with meats, or as a contrast to the heat of a spicy dish.
5. *Kongnamul*. Soybean sprouts blanched and seasoned with sesame, salt, and sometimes chili powder.

TAKE5 MARY CROWE'S TOP FIVE
KOREAN DISHES TO MAKE AT HOME

Mary Crowe has been writing about Korean food since 2003. She blogs at maryeats.com, and her work has appeared in *The Korea Times*, *The Korea Herald*, the LUXE Seoul city guide and *Korea Up Close*. A former Seoul resident, she now lives in Seattle where she is the Marketing and Community Relations Specialist for Whole Foods Market, Interbay.

No doubt after spending a few days in Korea, you've developed a taste for the local cuisine. Maybe it was the interplay between tangy, spicy and mild flavors, or the satisfying crunch of deep-fried nibbles. Heck, you might even leave addicted to chewy rice cakes. Regardless, preparing Korean meals at home is simple, and an Asian supermarket will have all the necessary ingredients, including chili paste, soy sauce and rice vinegar. Here are five Korean dishes to make at home.

1. **Seasoned Chili Paste**. One of my favorite Korean cookbooks, *Eating Korean*, by Cecilia Hae-Jin Lee, includes a recipe for seasoned chili paste. Simple and versatile, this sweet, sour, salty and spicy condiment is fantastic smeared on fish, chicken and meats, or used to top veggies and rice. www.eatingkorean.com/blog.

2. *Gyeranmari* (**a rolled omelet**). Manngchi's Korean Cooking is a popular Korean cooking website with fantastic step-by-step videos. You'll find a video recipe for near every Korean dish, plus a few fusion ones. *Gyeranmari* is one I find myself making over and over again -- it's an easy and light lunch or snack. www.maangchi.com.

3. **Cucumber Kimchi**. The recipe website epicurious.com features some of my Korean favorites, including a recipe for cucumber kimchi. Cooling, with a kiss of heat, I love to mix it up with rice noodles for a light summer lunch.

4. **Ssam**. Hands down my go-to meal in a pinch, *ssam* means "to wrap." All you need is some lettuce, condiments, rice and a vessel for leftovers. You'll find a recipe for "flat iron *ssam*" on my blog, www.maryeats.com.

5. *Tteok-guk* (**rice cake soup**). Traditionally served for the Lunar New Year. I'm addicted to the toothsome texture of the rice cakes and the homey chicken or beef stock. See www.maryeats.com for a recipe.

ROYAL CUISINE

Seasonality is at the heart of Korean culinary philosophy, except when it comes to royalty. Royal court cuisine features the finest specialties of each of the Korean Peninsula's regions or provinces. To please the king, five daily meals were prepared by an army of chefs, liquor makers and servants. Restaurants that specialize in royal court cuisine feature dishes such as *sinseollo*, a hot pot, and *pyeonsu*, boat shaped dumplings floating in ice, among other highly refined and labor intensive dishes. When in Korea, you still eat like a king!

Non-Korean Seoul Food

Seoul has long been famous for great food, but for most of its history that food was exclusively Korean, with some Japanese and Chinese dishes on offer.

Until quite recently, getting a good Italian or French meal outside of a few top hotels catering to foreigners was difficult. Moreover, red wine was hard to come by, and good bread near non-existent. All of that has changed dramatically.

Seoul has become increasingly popular with tourists and business people, and now maintains a large community of foreigners. The international dining scene has evolved correspondingly. It's not really outsiders, however, who are driving the cosmopolitan gourmet boom; it's Seoulites themselves, many of whom have visited, studied, or lived overseas and have brought back with them a taste for everything from burritos to kebabs to baguettes. Even Koreans who have not traveled abroad seem to know their way around a bowl of risotto or a glass of Burgundy.

Italian food is particularly popular in Seoul, and there are numerous casual and high-end restaurants offering pizza, as well as more sophisticated fare. Italian dishes also show up in restaurants specializing in "fusion" cuisine. This term is somewhat

TEA TIME

Tea drinking has been a part of Korea's culture since the seventh century. The most prized leaves come from the Boseong region in southern Korea.

Seoul's Insa-dong neighborhood is famous for Korean produced tea, as well as traditional tea houses and tea ceremonies. Green tea's antioxidant properties have made it a highly sought after ingredient, and you'll find it in Frappuccinos, ice cream, cake, cream puffs and wheat noodles. True green tea fanatics will want to sample *nokdon-*

open-ended, but generally involves mixing foods and cooking techniques from Asia, Europe and North America. Of course, "fusion" is just the age old practice of melding different cuisines, as seen in the kimchi burger sold at Lotteria, Korea's most popular fast food chain.

Fast food aside, there are many Korean chefs who are skilled in preparing foreign dishes (sometimes with an Asian touch, sometimes not). Seoul's trendier areas are also home to top-flight imported chefs and restaurateurs who bring the latest from the kitchens of Paris, Milan and Los Angeles to Korea.

For those craving a good old fashioned hamburger, they are certainly available, as are steaks, fries and other North American comfort foods. The standard global fast-food outlets -- McDonalds, KFC, Subway, Starbucks and Dunkin' Donuts -- are represented, as are full-service restaurant chains like Tony Roma's, Outback Steakhouse and T.G.I. Friday's.

It would be a shame to skip Korean food while in Seoul, but it certainly can be done, and done well at that. From kebabs ordered from an Itaewon storefront, to a trendy fusion meal in Gangnam, there is ample international cuisine to satisfy the visiting palate.

samgyeopsal, grilled pork belly from pigs that spend their days feasting on green tea leaves.

Coffee houses, both independent shops and those operated by Starbucks and the like, are a more recent addition to Seoul's caffeine culture. The chains are more reasonably priced, although many independent coffee places are prized for their atmosphere and innovative décor.

TAKE5 FIVE KOREAN
ALCOHOLIC BEVERAGES

1. **Soju**. Typically made from distilled sweet potatoes, this clear liquor is often compared to vodka. Goes down easy and fast, so proceed with caution. Soju cocktails are becoming popular in bars around Seoul. The "*soju* kettle" is a two-liter soda bottle that is chopped in half and contains its namesake mixed with fruit and lemon-lime soda.

2. **Baekseju**. Its name means "100 years wine," and *baekseju* is a rice liquor brewed with medicinal herbs, typically ginseng.

3. **Makgeolli**. Made from cooked and fermented rice, *makgeolli* has a milky appearance and a rustic taste. *Makgeolli* is a hearty, traditional beverage favored by farmers. You can sometimes spot hikers rewarding themselves with a glass or two after a grueling trek.

4. **Maekju**. Korean beer. Three similar-tasting, American-style, lager-esque beers dominate the Korean market: OB, Hite, and Cass. All work well at putting out fires induced by kimchi or spicy stir fries. One beer to look out for is Hite Stout, a darker, maltier beer.

5. **Fruit Wines**. Fruits are combined with alcohol for a sweet after-dinner cordial-like beverage. These drinks are typically taken in shots. *Maesilju* (plum wine) is most popular; grape and raspberry are other favorites.

6. **Sujeonggwa**. This one is a non-alcoholic, cinnamon and dried persimmon punch. The sweet drink is refreshing after a large meal.

DO NO HARM

Vegetarian cuisine is still under the radar in Seoul, but one way to ensure meatless meals is to dine in restaurants specializing in temple food. Buddhism was introduced to Korea over 1,600 years ago and set clear and strict culinary guidelines: No eating anything too spicy or salty, and nothing that will overstimulate or ignite the emotions. Found mostly in the tradition-oriented Insadong neighborhood, temple restaurants feature set meals of cruelty-free dining.

TAKE5 FIVE SEOUL STREET FOODS

Street vendors, known as *pojang-macha*, are found most everywhere in the city. Don't worry, the food is perfectly safe, although the newcomer may have a difficult time identifying the delicacies on the cart.

1. *Tteokbokki*. Chewy rice cakes simmered in a sweet spicy sauce with green onions and bite-sized fish cakes (odeng). The Korean equivalent of mac and cheese is enjoyed by children and adults.

2. *Gimbap*. Various fillings wrapped in rice and seaweed. The contents can include egg, carrots, blanched spinach, ham and radish.

3. *Sundae*. Korean sausage stuffed with sweet potato noodles, vegetables and congealed pork blood.

4. *Twigim*. The word means "deep-fried," and includes battered and fried vegetables, squid, and shrimp. Extra delicious when dipped in the accompanying *tteokbokki* sauce. *Mandu-twigim* (fried dumplings) and *yachae-twigim* (deep fried vegetables) are popular choices.

5. *Hotteok*. Dough stuffed with brown sugar and cooked on a griddle, like a pancake. These are popular in winter and invariably consumed quickly – better get two.

TO YOUR HEALTH!

Unlike in the West where people greedily grab bottles and pour their own drinks, in Korea you pour for someone else and he or she will do likewise. Custom also dictates that one should use two hands—particularly if being served by an older person—one to hold the receiving cup (or offering bottle) and the second resting under the wrist or elbow. It is also considered polite to stand slightly and bow once a senior person has poured your drink.

TAKE 5 FIVE COMMON DRINKING SNACKS

1. *Fried Chicken*. Forget what you know about fried chicken. Korean fried chicken gets its addictive crispy texture from a two-part Asian frying technique. The chicken is dredged lightly in flour, then coated in a delicate batter and fried at a low temperature. It is then removed from the fryer and allowed to rest before being returned to the oil for an additional ten minutes. This process turns the skin into an irresistibly thin, crackly crust. The perfect complement to a frosty beer.

2. *Dubu*-kimchi. Slabs of cottony tofu are steamed and stir fried with *baechu*-kimchi. A great spicy complement to the liquor table.

3. *Jokbal*. Pig's feet cooked in a soy sauce, sugar, and garlic glaze, and then chilled and sliced thin. Served with a dipping sauce.

4. *Pajeon*. Uncut green onions, and sometimes shellfish, are placed on a thin layer of savory batter in a pan and cooked to roughly the size of a hubcap. Served with a vinegar soy sauce for dipping.

5. *Nakjibokkeum*. Octopus is cut into bite-sized pieces and tossed with red-pepper garlic sauce. It is then stir-fried over high heat with onions, green peppers and carrots.

Did you know. . .

that metal chopsticks, as opposed to wood or plastic ones, are commonly used in Korea? Metal chopsticks are durable, and are ecologically superior to disposable wooden sticks. However, metal chopsticks are slipperier than their wooden counterparts, and so a little harder to manipulate, particularly for the uninitiated.

Weblinks

Seoul City Tourism
www.visitseoul.net
Click on the "Lodging and Dining" tab.

Korea Tourism
www.visitkorea.or.kr
Download "The Wonderful World of Korean Food" e-book under the "Before You Come" section of the English language homepage.

Institute of Korean Royal Cuisine
www.food.co.kr/english/01.html

Seoul Eats
www.seouleats.com
A lively site with plentiful photographs covering Korean and global cuisine in Seoul, as well as social trends and aspects of daily life in Seoul.

ZenKimchi Korean Food Journal
www.zenkimchi.com
Korean food blog with recipes, reviews and reader comments. Plenty for the curious and adventuresome.

Institute of Korean Traditional Food
www.kfr.or.kr
A government sponsored institute devoted to promoting Korean food and culture.

Language & Beliefs

Where the Korean language came from and what it is related to are mysterious. Korean is completely distinct from neighboring tongues like Chinese, Japanese and Russian.

At one time Korean was believed to be part of the Ural-Altaic language group, which includes Finnish and Hungarian, but that theory has lost currency. Another theory holds that Korean is a member of the Altaic language group along with the Turkic languages and Mongolian. Still others deem Korean a language isolate, meaning it has no genealogical relationship with any other tongue.

Regardless of its origins, Korean is a challenging language for foreigners. Korean employs a subject-object-verb syntax. English, on the other hand, uses a subject-verb-object structure, as in "Sheila washes the car."

This basic difference in sentence structure, among other things, is why English speakers typically find Korean difficult to learn. The Defense Language Institute (operated by the U.S. Department of Defense) classifies Korean as a Category IV language, meaning it is among the hardest for an English native speaker to learn. In practice, a student learning the Korean language requires more than twice as long to attain a limited working level of proficiency in it than does one studying French or Italian.

Korean is difficult, but not impossible, and an increasing number of foreigners are learning the language. Moreover, Korean script, which is known as Hangeul, is completely phonetic and can be learned quite quickly.

HANGEUL

When Hangeul or Korean script (as opposed to *Hanguk-mal* or Korean speech) was first formulated in the fifteenth century, it contained 28 letters. Over time, four letters have been dropped. Modern Hangeul has 10 vowels and 14 consonants. Hangeul is often called an alphabet, but it is really a language of syllables since neither the vowels nor consonants can stand on their own.

A vowel needs a consonant to be pronounced, and vice versa. There are no single letter words such as "I" or "a," and groups of consonants such as "psst" cannot be pronounced in Korean without vowels.

Hangeul's 14 consonants and 10 vowels combine to form syllable blocks. For example, the word "Hangeul" (한글) would be constructed as follows:

한 (han) = ㅎ (h) + ㅏ (a) + ㄴ (n)
글 (geul) = ㄱ (g) + ㅡ (eu) + ㄹ (l)

Traditionally, Korean text was written vertically in columns reading from right to left. However, in most contemporary novels, newspapers and magazines, text is written in rows reading from left to right.

They said it

"The best alphabet one can dream of."
  – writer John Man describing Hangeul in his 2000 book *Alpha Beta: How Our Alphabet Shaped the Western World*. Years earlier, Pearl Buck, author of *The Good Earth*, called Hangeul "the simplest, yet most advanced character set in the world."

THE HISTORY OF HANGEUL

Hangeul was invented in 1443 by King Sejong the Great, the fourth king of the Joseon Kingdom. Some scholars suspect that Hangeul was actually the work of a team of researchers rather than the king himself, but historical records show that the project was kept secret from the king's staff of scholars. Sejong may have been assisted by his sons;

TAKE5 FIVE ESSENTIAL KOREAN EXPRESSIONS

1. Hello; How do you do? 안녕하세요? *An-nyeong-ha-se-yo?*

This is the most common greeting in Korean. It literally means "Are you at peace?" or "Is all well with you?" Typically, you respond and pose the same question, i.e., first you would say "*Ne*" ("Yes"), and then ask "*An-nyeong-ha-se-yo?*"

2. Can you speak English? 영어를 할 수 있어요? *Yeong-eo-reul hal ssu i-sseo-yo?*

This is an expression that is invaluable to the traveler who doesn't speak much Korean. Hopefully, the person asked will answer in the affirmative by saying "*Ne*" ("Yes"), rather than "*Aniyo*" ("No").

3. Thank you 감사합니다 *Gam-sa-ham-ni-da.*

This is the polite way to express your thanks when given a gift or a compliment. Good manners in any country can go a long way.

4. I'm sorry 미안합니다 *Mi-an-ham-ni-da.*

Use this expression to express regret for having done something offensive, or for having made a mistake of some kind. It is used in a narrow sense only when you feel you have done something wrong.

5. How much is this? 이거 얼마예요? *I-geo eol-ma-ye-yo?*

If you plan on shopping in Korea, you are going to need this expression. 이거(*I-geo*) means "This thing," something that you have in your hand. If you point to something away from you and want to know the price, just replace 이거(*I-geo*) with 저거(*Jeo-geo*) and say "*Jeo-geo eol-ma-ye-yo?*" ("How much is that?"). Korean merchants will often punch the number into a calculator and hold it up for you.

regardless, Hangeul was obviously a very personal project for him.

The complete writing system was first published in a 1446 document entitled *Hunmin Jeong-eum*, or "Proper Sounds for the Instruction of the People." In the work's preface, King Sejong stated his reasons for creating an indigenous script: "Being of foreign origin, Chinese characters are incapable of capturing uniquely Korean meanings. Therefore, many common people have no way to express their thoughts and feelings. Out of my sympathy for their difficulties, I have created a set of 28 letters. The letters are very easy to learn, and it is my fervent hope that they improve the quality of life of all people."

Hangeul is now considered by many to be the world's simplest, yet most scientific writing system. Until the early twentieth century, however, Hangeul was denigrated by the Korean literati, many of whom preferred the traditional *Hanja* or Chinese character writing system.

To express their scorn for Hangeul, some elites gave it derogatory names such as *Amgeul* (women's script), *Atgeul* (children's script) and *Achimgeul* (writing that can be learned in one morning). The modern name Hangeul was coined in 1912 by Korean linguist Ju Si-Gyeong. *Han* can mean "great" or "Korean," and *geul* is the Korean word for "script."

Hangeul is a source of national pride for Koreans. Hangeul Day is celebrated on October 9 in South Korea, and it commemorates King Sejong's publication of the alphabet system. The Korean language is no longer just for Koreans; since 1997, the Korean language has been an optional foreign language subject on the U.S. Scholastic Achievement Test, and the Korean proficiency test can be taken in many countries including Japan, China, Kazakhstan and Uzbekistan.

Did you know. . .

that the Korean alphabet has been adopted as the official script of the Cia-Cia tribe of Bau-Bau city in southeastern Indonesia? The Cia-Cia tribe numbers about 80,000 people, and has no native writing system. Fearing the disappearance of their language, they have adopted Hangeul to transcribe their native tongue.

KOREAN NAMES

Most Korean names are made up of three syllables comprising three Chinese characters with distinct meanings. The pattern is typically a one-syllable paternal lineage family name called "*seong,*" followed by a two-syllable given name called "*ireum.*" For example, the name of the South Korean President is Lee Myung-bak; his family name is "Lee." There are fewer than 300 Korean family names in use today, and several are extremely common. The names "Kim," "Lee" or "Yi," and "Park" account for 45 percent of all Korean family names.

Korean given names are often made up of a one-character generation name called *dollimja*, plus a unique one character name. Each member of the same generation in the extended family will have one character that is the same, and one that is unique to that individual. Two brothers or cousins of the same generation might have given names such as "Hyeon-jun" and "Seok-jun," where "jun" would be the common generation character, and "Hyeon" or "Seok" the unique individual character.

Korean women traditionally keep their family name after marriage, and while given names for women sometimes follow the *dollimja* system, it's not as common as it is for males. In fact, contemporary parents often give their children names that are derived from native Korean words such as *haneul* (sky).

Unless they are close friends, Koreans rarely call each other by

Did you know. . .

that the number four (*sa*) is considered bad luck in Korea because it has the same sound as the Chinese character for death? Consequently, many buildings in Korea don't have a fourth floor, and those that do often replace "4" with the letter "F" on the elevator button.

Confucianism and Hangeul

Confucianism was the moral compass of Korean life for over 500 years, and it outlined a strict social hierarchy. It called for the subordination of the son to the father, the younger to the elder, the wife to the husband and the subject to the throne. Confucianism is no longer widely practiced in Korea, however it still exerts influence over the language.

There are several levels of speech in Korean, each having different verb endings. A speaker can show his superiority as far as social position or age by speaking down or using "*banmal*," the non-honorific form of speech.

This kind of speech might be used by a father to his son, or by a boss to his subordinates. Conversely, the superiority of the listener can be acknowledged by using "*jondaenmal*," or respectful speech. This would be used by a student speaking to his teacher, or a new employee speaking to his superior. A person can also show respect by lowering himself. For example, when speaking to a subordinate or equal, a person might refer to him or herself using "*Na*" (I/me). When addressing a superior or elder, however, "*Jeo*," a more humble form of I/me, would be employed.

Vocabulary choice is another way to show respect. There are some sets of Korean words that have the same basic meaning, but which differentiate the social level of the speaker and the listener. The different names given rice, or a meal in general, are a good example. The general term for rice is "bap"; a more respectful or formal word is "*siksa*," and an even more polite term is "*jin-ji*." The corresponding verbs meaning "eat" are also different, and can be further modified to fit the situation by changing the verb endings.

For someone not familiar with Confucianism and different levels of speech, Korean can be daunting. Where it really gets confusing is when you are speaking to your father about your grandfather. Generally, it is better to err on the side of caution by being overly formal, rather than showing disrespect by being too casual.

their given names. It's common to refer to someone by their title, as in "Director Kim," or "Superintendent Lee," or by terms such as "Uncle" or "Sister." Parents are usually called by the name of their eldest son or daughter. For example, if the eldest son's name is Hyeon-jun, the mother would be called "Hyeon-jun's mom" and the father "Hyeon-jun's dad."

TAKE 5 FIVE KOREAN IDIOMS

1. **The sky is high and the horses are fat.** 천고마비 *cheon-go-ma-bi.*
This refers to autumn or harvest time when the blue skies seem to stretch for forever, and food is abundant (for livestock and people).

2. **Give the disease then give the remedy.** 병 주고 약 준다 *byeong ju-go yak jun-da.*
This proverb refers to someone who causes you harm, and then tries to make you feel better. An example would be a person who, after spreading a rumor about you that sparks a fight with your significant other, then offers a shoulder to cry on.

3. **Eat mustard and cry.** 울며 겨자 먹기 *ul-myeo gyeo-ja meok-kki.*
The mustard referenced here is so hot that it makes you cry. This saying is used when you have to do something that you really don't want to. It's similar to the English idiom "Suck it up."

4. **Hunger is a sidedish.** 시장이 반찬이다 *si-jang-i ban-cha-ni-da.*
A basic Korean meal consists of a bowl of rice and several sidedishes. Since the rice is always the same, it's the sidedishes that make the meal tasty. The implication is that when you are hungry, anything tastes good.

5. **Extract and eat the liver of a flea.** 벼룩의 간을 빼먹다 *byeo-ru-gui ga-neul ppae-meok-tta.*
Extracting the liver from a flea would take great time and effort, and the result would hardly be worth eating. This expression is used to describe the actions of someone, like a tax collector, who tries to get something from a person who has little or nothing.

TRADITIONAL NICKNAMES

During the Joseon Kingdom (1392-1910) Confucianism was an integral part of daily life. A wife had the duty of producing a male heir who would carry on the husband's bloodline, take care of the couple in their old age, and perform ancestral rites after their deaths. Korean women would pray to various spirits for a son, sometimes invoking the

TAKE 5 FIVE MEMORABLE KOREAN
PHONE NUMBERS

The sounds of Korean numbers result in many puns and associations, including the following commercial applications.

1. **Trains**. When the numbers 7 and 8 are combined, as in 7788 (*chil-chil-pal-pal*), it sounds like a train pulling from a station. If you dial a local number ending in 7788, you will likely get the railroad administration.

2. **Pizza delivery**. Domino's pizza is known for its fast delivery; if the pizza doesn't arrive in 30 minutes, it's free. That's why in Korea, Domino's last four numbers are 3082. The 30 suggests thirty minutes, and the 8-2 sounds like the Korean word "*ppal-li*," meaning "quickly."

3. **Dentists**. The numbers 2-8 (*i-pal*) sound like the Korean word for teeth, and 7-5 sounds like the Korean word for "cure" or "treatment." A number ending in 2875 is therefore ideal for a dentist. Another popular such number is 2828 (*i-pal-i-pal*) or "teeth-teeth."

4. **A Firing range**. One way to say "zero" in Korean is *bbang*; a number ending in 0000 ("*bbang-bbang-bbang-bbang*") sounds like a gun firing shots.

5. **Movers**. The number 2 (*i*) and number 4 (*sa*), when said together, sound like the verb "to move" (i-sa), as in moving into a new house or apartment. For this reason, the phone number for Korean moving companies often ends in 2424.

"*Samsin-halmeoni*," a spirit in the form of a grandmother.

The birth of a son was considered a blessing, but if rewarded with such a gift, family members were careful not to praise the child too much, or speak of its good health, beauty, strength or intelligence. They believed that doing so would arouse jealousy in the gods, who might then harm the boy. This belief was likely rooted in the high rate of infant and child mortality of the day. To ensure that young male children were not taken by jealous gods, the family would give boys humbling or derogatory nicknames.

KONGLISH

English loan words found their way into the Korean language as early as the end of the nineteenth century. Many of these terms have had their pronunciation and meanings Koreanized, and have come to be known as Konglish, a mix of Korean and English. There are also Konglish words which came into the Korean language via Japanese, and have therefore gone through more than one transformation, making them unrecognizable to the native English speaker.

English words that end in a voiced consonant or "s" are hard to pronounce in Korean; often a short vowel sound like a *schwa* is added, creating an extra syllable. A word like "had" would be pronounced

Did you know. . .

that in Korea blood type is seen by many as an important influence on personality and character? Similar to the belief in astrology in the West, "blood type theory" associates particular blood types with traits such as introversion/extroversion, individuality/conformity and emotionality/rationality. There have been books, movies and songs written on the topic, including the popular 2005 romantic comedy *My Boyfriend is Type-B*.

"hae-deu," and "is" as "i-jeu." There are also some sounds that just don't exist in Korean such as "th," "f," "v," and "z." And if that isn't enough, the letter "r" cannot be distinguished from the letter "l" in Korean words. Considering the many differences in pronunciation between English and Korean, Hangeul does a pretty good job of mimicking English sounds.

The following table presents a selection of words imported into Korean from English. Some of the words have taken a strange trip indeed, and have strayed substantially from their original English meaning.

English Root	Korean Pronunciation	Meaning in Korea	Hangeul
gagman	gae-geu-maen	a comedian	개그맨
level up	re-be-reop	to upgrade, raise the level	레벨업
manicure	mae-ni-kyu-eo	nail polish	매니큐어
meeting	mi-ting	a blind date	미팅
pants	ppan-seu	underwear	빤스
back number	baeng-neom-beo	a jersey number	백넘버
sharp pencil	sya-peu-pen-seul	a mechanical pencil	샤프펜슬
service	seo-bi-seu	free, on the house	서비스
stand	seu-taen-deu	a desk lamp	스탠드
eye shopping	a-i-syo-ping	window shopping	아이쇼핑
over eat	o-ba-i-teu	to throw up	오바이트
old miss	ol-deu mi-seu	a spinster or old maid	올드 미스
white shirt	wa-i-syeo-cheu	a dress shirt	와이셔츠
training	chu-ri-ning	a sweat suit, a jogging suit	추리닝
cunning	keon-ning	cheating (as on an exam)	컨닝

talent	tael-leon-teu	a TV star, an entertainer	탤런트
perm	pa-ma	a hair perm	파마
hard (ice cream)	ha-deu	a popsicle	하드
handphone	haen-deu-pon	a mobile or cell phone	핸드폰
fighting	hwa-i-ting	You can do it! Way to go!	화이팅

Shamanism

Sometimes known as animism, shamanism holds that there are spirits in mountains, trees and other objects. Prior to the advent of Buddhism and Christianity, shamanism was the dominant mode of spiritual belief in Korea.

The shaman, or priest, acts as intermediary between the everyday and spirit worlds. The role of the shaman is to reconcile the spirit and human spheres; this is accomplished by communicating with the spirits using a series of rituals that employ intense chanting and frenzied dancing.

Shamanistic beliefs, and the practices of shaman priests, were discouraged and even outlawed during the Confucianist Joseon Kingdom. This prohibition continued during the period of Japanese rule, and to a lesser extent in the years after the Korean War when folk practices were frowned upon as detrimental to Korea's modernization.

Shamanism is now recognized as a long standing element of Korean culture, and has experienced something of a revival. Many Koreans view shamanism as superstitious or primitive, but shamans are still practicing and are sometimes consulted by Koreans during times of need. Many Koreans, even if they are not adherents of shamanism, recognize the cultural and historic value of the tradition, and its practice is now more open than it has been in some time.

TAKE5 DAVID A. MASON'S TOP FIVE
SEOUL TEMPLES

David A. Mason is a Professor of Korean Tourism at Seoul's Kyung Hee University, and a researcher on the religious character of Korea's mountains. A U.S. citizen, he has lived in Korea for 25 years, and has authored six books on Korean culture and tourism, including *Spirit of the Mountains* and *Passage to Korea*. His popular website on sacred Korean mountains and their spirits can be found at www.san-shin.org.

1. Doseon-sa on Samgak-san in Gangbuk-gu

This is probably the largest, most historic and most religiously important temple in Seoul. Founded by great National-Master Doseon more than a millennium ago, it is a treasure of his *pungsu-jiri* (Korean Geomancy), and features his own monumental carving of the Bodhisattva of Compassion. It also contains unique memorials to key figures of the twentieth century revival of Korean Buddhism, and offers magnificent views of Mt. Samgak's mighty peaks, and of the trailheads leading toward them.

2. Inwang-sa on Inwang-san in Jongno-gu

Inwang-sa is really a complex of Buddhist temples and shamanic shrines that are gradually becoming regarded as a single temple. They are clustered around the amazing *Seon-bawi* (Sacred-Boulder), and the profound Guksa-dang national-spirits shrine, and together offer visitors fantastic icons, altars and demonstrations of indigenous Korean spirituality. The upper areas of this temple-complex provide amazing views of downtown Seoul.

3. Bongeun-sa in Gangnam-gu

This is a peaceful, interesting and easily accessible oasis right in the middle of the metropolis's wealthiest madness (near the COEX complex). It features excellent artworks and a large standing Mireuk Buddha statue, and remains a historic center of translation and teaching. This temple has also done very well in developing its temple-stay programs, and is remarkably welcoming to international visitors.

4. Bongwon-sa on An-san in Seodaemun-gu

This is a large, historic and colorful temple that serves as the head-quarters of the Taego Order of Korean Buddhism. It features some of the best *dancheong* paintings on the outside of its buildings, and *taenghwa* paintings inside them. These were accomplished or supervised by the late Manbong Seunim, a great national master of Buddhist painting-arts. It also features lovely landscaping, some good statues and authentic performances of Korea's Buddhist music and dance.

5. Seungga-sa on Bi-bong in Jongno-gu

This is one of the few remaining temples that is accessible only by hiking up steep trails, and here the trek is most well-rewarded. Near the crest of the front-range-line of Samgak-san, below a couple of the most prominent peaks of Bukhan-san National Park, it features an amazing modern pagoda, an ancient cliff-carved Buddha, and excellent painted icons in the Halls tucked between gigantic granite boulders and twisted pine trees.

RELIGION

About 53 percent of South Koreans are adherents of a religious faith. Of those specifying a religion, the dominant faiths are Buddhism (43 percent), Protestantism (35 percent) and Catholicism (21 percent). There are many Protestant denominations represented, and Korea has proved fertile ground for both Protestant and Catholic missionaries.

TAKE5 FIVE BOOKS EXPLAINING KOREAN CULTURE AND SOCIETY

1. *Ugly Koreans, Ugly Americans. Cultural and Behavioral Differences between Koreans and Americans* by **Min Byoung-chul, Ed.D.** BCM Media, Inc. 2004, 195 pages, paperback. A compact, bilingual book with cartoon illustrations which explains attitudes and customs that may baffle or upset Americans about Koreans, and vice-versa. An amusing and easy to read treatment of cultural differences.

2. *Notes on Things Korean* by **Suzanne Crowder Han.** Hollym, 1995, 248 pages. Short pieces on elements of traditional Korean culture including holidays, games, historic figures, arts and crafts, beliefs, customs, music and dance.

3. *Understanding Koreans and Their Culture* by **Choi Joon-sik, Ph.D.** HER ONE MEDIA, 2007, 232 pages, paperback. The role of religion and Confucianism, as well as "spontaneity" and "ecstasy," in traditional and contemporary Korean culture, art and society are explored in this thoughtful book.

4. *Korea Bug: The Best of a Zine that Infected a Nation* by **J. Scott Burgeson.** Eunhaeng Namu Press, 2005, 374 pages, paperback. Off-beat and irreverent interviews, commentary, essays and comics about local characters, the 1990s 'zine scene and miscellaneous aspects of contemporary Korean culture and society. Selected from issues of Burgeson's *Korea Bug* 'zine originally published between 1997 and 2001.

5. *The 48 Keywords that Describe Korea.* GONGTO KOREA, 2006, 125 pages, paperback. Forty-eight important words and phrases ranging from "Plastic Surgery Craze," "Well-Being Trend," and "Admiral Lee Sun-Shin," to "Samsung Electronics," "Blood Type Theory Boom," and "Mixed Martial Arts" are explained in this small volume.

Attending religious services is common in Korea, and unlike North America and Europe where there is a shortage of religious workers, Korea actually "exports" Catholic priests and Protestant missionaries to countries in need.

Confucianism also plays an important part in Korea. Confucianism is a set of ethical and cultural precepts that was dominant during the Joseon Kingdom. Not many Koreans today would call themselves "Confucianists," yet certainly they are influenced by Confucian beliefs, a number of which have proved compatible with Christianity.

Seoul has a number of mega-churches, notably the Yeouido Full Gospel Church which has 763,000 members (it started in 1958 with a mere five adherents) and 600 missionaries. The Full Gospel Church's various Sunday services attract over 200,000 worshippers throughout the day. In addition to the Full Gospel Church, Seoul is home to the largest Methodist and the largest Presbyterian churches in the world. In addition to the big churches, there are the thousands of smaller ones. Seoul's night sky is lit up with a plethora of red neon crosses; some are from free-standing churches, but many come from anonymous mid-rises where a tiny church occupying a few rooms might hold services for a few dozen faithful.

South Korea is notable for its religious tolerance. Despite all the travails that have occurred on the Korean Peninsula over the centuries, battles over religion have been rare. Perhaps the unifying force of repelling outside influence and domination, and the ongoing tension with North Korea, has made religious differences less important than they might otherwise be to South Koreans.

Did you know. . .

that there is a Korean Fortune Tellers Association? Fortune telling is still practiced in Korea, although of late the psychics have been besieged with questions about the economy, rather than relationships. Korea's fortune tellers are increasingly professional and tend to specialize in particular areas. They are also well acquainted with e-commerce and on-line marketing of their services.

GINSENG

Korean ginseng is world famous for its stamina and vitality boosting properties, as well as its salutary effects on digestion and the immune system. It might not be a cure-all, but most Koreans will tell you that a shot of ginseng is bound to help fix what ails you.

Ginseng has a distinctive earthy, bitter taste, which is sometimes ameliorated with honey or other sweeteners. Korean ginseng is expensive, which is not surprising as it is difficult to grow, takes years to mature, and requires particular soil and weather conditions. The plant is found in its wild state in remote mountainous areas, and has been cultivated for centuries.

Buyers should be beware — look for the "Korea Insam" seal which shows that the product was grown in Korea. Imports from China and elsewhere are different varieties of ginseng and rarely measure up. Ginseng is available in areas popular with visitors, like Insadong and Itaewon, as well as in many department stores and markets. True connoisseurs may want to head to the Gyeongdong Herbal Medicine Market, which has over 1,000 stalls selling all manner of plants, roots and tinctures designed to cure one ailment or another. The sprawling Namdaemun Market is another good place for purchasing ginseng.

It is illegal to take raw untreated ginseng out of the country, but *hongsam*, or "red ginseng," which is steamed and then dried, may be removed. If you don't wish to buy the root itself, a vast array of packaged ginseng tablets, powders, liquid extracts and capsules are available for purchase. There are also ginseng teas, candies and jellies. Like kimchi, ginseng is steeped in lore and tradition, and is a true made-in-Korea staple.

Did you know. . .

that in Korea it's considered a unwise to buy a lover shoes as a present? Doing so is thought to be bad luck as it suggests that the sweetheart will run off and find someone else.

They said it

"Korea has for some time taken pride in its claims to be one of the world's few ethnically homogeneous nations. As time passes, however, the nation's claims to ethnic homogeneity have grown increasingly tenuous. A powerful combination of increasing globalization and stark demographic trends has led to a growing internationalization of Korean society. There can be no denying that the face of Korea is changing - quite literally."

– Seoul writer and editor Robert Koehler

WELL BEING

One of the most popular social trends in Korea in the 2000s was the "well-being" movement. The principle is simple: People should slow down, eat healthier food and live more balanced lives. Essentially, the well-being ideal holds that taking care of one's body and attaining spiritual and psychological peace are more important than material goods or success narrowly defined. The movement initially seemed to be a needed antidote to the pressure of life in fast-paced Seoul, but soon there were complaints that "well-being" was itself becoming a marketing strategy. Organic food stores and yoga classes were logical manifestations of the trend, but department stores, banks and other businesses also sought to ride the well-being wave.

BE MY VALENTINE

In Korea, it is customary for women to give chocolate to men on Valentine's Day, but not the converse. In addition to February 14, there are a number of light-hearted, commerce driven "days," most of which are geared toward young people. These include White Day (March 14) when men give gifts and candies to their lovers, and Black Day (April 14). Black Day is for singles who came up empty on Valentine's or White Day. The lonely hearts "celebrate" by wearing black and then going out to eat black noodles. Pepero Day (November 11) is popular among students who give each other Pepero, long thin stick biscuits that are dipped in chocolate. November 11, or 11-11, looks like 4 Pepero sticks.

Arts & Entertainment

Seoul's arts and entertainment life encompasses everything from lively festivals, theme parks and nightclubs to world-class museums and performances of *pansori* and *sanjo* (ancient Korean musical forms). The city is a paradise for culture vultures, night owls, art lovers, music buffs and anyone who just likes to get out and have a good time.

Korean traditional and folk art, including ceramics, paper and textiles, are known the world over for their elegance, beauty and craftsmanship. The art scene is such that it also features a number of innovative museums devoted to contemporary Korean and foreign art. The museum buildings — some of them classics, others newfangled creations by "starchitects" like Rem Koolhaas — are worth the trip alone, never mind what is inside.

Koreans are music lovers, and Seoul is home to elegant venues presenting indigenous Korean music and dance. The National Center for Korean Traditional Performing Arts, Korea House and Seoul Namsan Gugakdang, among others, are more than just concert halls; they are lovingly designed traditional cultural spaces. Seoul is also a world center for Western classical music, and lovers of pop, rock, dance and jazz music have lots to choose from here.

In the 1990s Seoul became a hotbed for contemporary music, film and television. The Seoul-born *hallyu*, or "Korean Wave," swept Japan and Southeast Asia in the early 2000s and is now lapping at the shores of countries worldwide. This Korean-produced entertainment explosion has also become big business. Seoul has joined the ranks of cities like Tokyo, Mumbai, Los Angeles, New York and London, where sales of culture and entertainment products are important sources of economic activity. You can even sample some of this "wave" from abroad as popular Korean television dramas, movies, novels and comics are all available overseas.

Seoulites and Koreans also love sports. Seoul is famous, of course, for hosting the 1988 Summer Olympics, and was one of the sites for the 2002 World Cup. In addition to these global marquee events, Seoul has a number of professional sports teams, and is well endowed with athletic and recreational facilities.

Whether your preference is taking part in a street festival, cheering on the home team at a soccer or baseball game, riding a roller coaster, enjoying a late-night drink, listening to live music or getting lost in a museum, there is always something to do in Seoul. The problem isn't finding something to do, it's finding the time.

BY THE NUMBERS
- City festivals: 120
- Cultural assets: 1,290
- Museums: 106
- Theaters: 178
- Performing arts centers: 186
- Performances: 31,245 yearly
- Movie theaters: 73 (443 screens)

CITY OF FESTIVALS
Seoul hosts countless festivals celebrating everything from food, fashion and traditional culture to music, technology and sports. Hi Seoul is the biggest of the bunch, but there are many others. Chances are that if you are visiting Seoul, there is a festival going on somewhere.

They said it

"Seoul has pulled off the neat trick of becoming the dominant pop culture influence in Asia – even luring the fan base of its great rival Japan – and combined this with a knack for big business and cutting-edge design and technology."

— **Wallpaper* City Guide Seoul, 2008**

Hi Seoul Festival

Seoul's biggest party stretches over ten days in May. It is held at multiple venues about the city including the Han River parks, Seoul Plaza and Gwanghwamun Square. Organized around five concepts (Spectacles, Harmony, Dance, Fun and Art) the festival is a celebration of traditional and contemporary art, culture and entertainment.

Hi Seoul features everything from large-scale variety shows and concerts (classical, traditional, jazz and rock) to dance performances, fireworks, extreme sports and outdoor theater. There is something for everyone, from massive hi-tech events to simple street performances enjoyed by an audience of a few dozen. Hi Seoul is the city's signature event and it attracts millions of attendees from around the country and around the world. www.hiseoulfest.org

Seoul Fashion Week

Twice a year—in March and October—Seoul rolls out the red carpet for fashion's superstars. A jam-packed series of fashion shows, fairs, trade events and industry hobnobs, Seoul Fashion Week is a chance for fashion bigwigs to connect with industry buyers, the media and the public. It all goes down at the Seoul Trade Exhibition & Convention Center (SETEC) near Daechi station in southern Seoul. www.seoul-fashionweek.com.

The Seoul International Fireworks Festival

Each September, the sky above Yeouido Island in central Seoul explodes with a mind-blowing array of pyrotechnics. Not content to put on a mere show, the festival invites teams from around the world to compete for best performance.

Weaving choreographed music, video, lasers, and even water-art segments into their routines, these displays take fireworks to a new level. The fun begins at one p.m. with children's face-painting, balloon art and folk bands at the Han River Park grounds near the 63 City building. The skies light up around eight p.m. Check local papers or www.visitseoul.net for details.

Lotus Lantern Festival

The Lotus Lantern Festival is held in May to coincide with Buddha's birthday, and takes place in and around two of the capital's temples. The festival starts with a week-long display at Bongeunsa Temple of exquisitely colored, lighted lanterns.

A Sunday street festival invites visitors to make lanterns, listen to Buddhist music, taste temple food and participate in other traditional activities. The climax is the Lantern Parade, where scores of wondrous illuminated elephant, phoenix and dragon floats, and more than 100,000 individual lanterns, are marched through downtown Seoul's main drag after sundown. www.llf.or.kr/eng

Jongmyo Shrine Royal Ancestral Rites

During the Joseon era, these sacred rites took place five times a year as a way of honoring the kingdom's queens and kings. Now held once a year on the first Sunday in May, these elaborate ceremonies involve priests in ritual dress making offerings of special foods and wines to the spirits of Koreans' ancestors. The daylong rites are accompanied by traditional music and dances representing *eum* and yang forces. The Jongmyo Shrine is near Jongno 3-ga station, exit 11, on subway line 1. www.visitkorea.or.kr

Seoul Drum Festival

This nighttime bang-fest has been pounding away since 1999 and takes place in September. The festival has earned a reputation for attracting talented and varied performers. It's no surprise, then, that it has moved several times in search of more spacious digs: from downtown's City Hall Plaza, to the Han River parklands and, most recently, to Seoul Forest. Percussionists from several countries, as well as Korean traditional *samulnori* and "fusion" drum bands, battle it out for lucrative prize money. Visit www.drumfestival.org for details on dates and location.

TAKE5 TOP FIVE KOREAN FILMS
AT THE BOX OFFICE

1. *The Host* (2006): 13 million admissions. A Han River monster captures a young girl; her family tries to save her before it's too late.
2. *The King and the Clown* (2005): 12.3 million admissions. A crazy, bloodthirsty king falls in love with a male entertainer who often plays female roles.
3. *Taegukgi: The Brotherhood of War* (2004): 11.7 million admissions. A tale of two brothers trying to protect each other during the Korean War.
4. *Haeundae* (2009): 11.3 million admissions. A disaster epic in which a giant tsunami hits Haeundae, a famous beach on Korea's southeastern coast.
5. *Silmido* (2003): 11.1 million admissions. Thirty-one South Korean prisoners are given a pardon under the condition that they go on a suicide mission to kill the North Korean president. When the mission is called off, things get really complicated. The story was loosely based on real-life events.

Source: Korean Film Council 2009

TAKE5 FIVE LEADING VENUES
FOR TRADITIONAL PERFORMANCES

1. **The National Center for Korean Traditional Performing Arts.** The NCKTPA traces its lineage to the Silla Kingdom's Royal Institute of Music. Featuring a range of traditional styles, the NCTKPA is an outstanding place to hear authentic and historic Korean music, along with new compositions in traditional styles. There are regular Saturday performances as well as special concerts. The center also includes the Museum of Traditional Korean Music, whose impressive collection includes massive gold bells. www.gugak.go.kr.

2. **Korea House.** Located near Namsan Mountain, the Korea House complex transports visitors back to the time of the Joseon Kingdom. Once inside Korea House's gates, you'll find an elegant traditional village, an outdoor theater, an indoor performing arts space and a traditional goods gallery. Korea House presents dance and song performances, as well as actual (and re-enacted) traditional Korean weddings. Korea House is also a leading place to sample royal cuisine. www.koreahouse.or.kr.

3. **Samcheonggak.** Located in the forested mountains near the Blue House (the South Korean presidential residence) in northern Seoul, Samcheonggak is an enchanting spot. It was founded in 1972 as a traditional entertainment venue for high-ranking government officials. Samcheonggak's concerts are organized by the Sejong Center, and it contains a performance hall, a traditional Korean restaurant and a tea house. www.samcheonggak.or.kr/.

4. **Seoul Namsan Gugakdang.** Seoul Namsan Gugakdang is located inside Namsan Hanok Village. The concert hall was completed in 2007, and its lighting, sound and stage were constructed to provide the best acoustics and atmosphere specifically for Korean classical music concerts. The Namsan Gugakdang's program is organized by the Sejong Center, and in addition to special performances on weekends, it offers weekly Wednesday and Friday performances. Tickets are reasonably priced. www.sejongpac.or.kr/sngad

5. **Chongdong Theater.** This theater has made traditional music accessible to a broad audience, including foreigners with little background in the area. A single show takes the listener through interesting and illuminating examples of the representative styles. Very friendly and visitor-oriented. www.mct.or.kr.

Seoul International Cartoon & Animation Festival (SICAF)

This quirky summer festival introduces the newest trends in animation technology and technique, and is a networking event for Asian animation industry movers and shakers. Each year celebrates a unique aspect of Korea's cartoon/animation scene; the 2009 fest included an animation film festival and a trip down memory lane celebrating the 100th anniversary of *manhwa* (Korean comics). Visit www.sicaf.org for venue details and dates.

Seoul Fringe Festival

With no formal screening process, the Seoul Fringe Festival (or just "Fringe") gives artists of all genres a chance to experiment in the theaters, parks, basement clubs, streets and sidewalks of western Seoul's artsy Hongdae neighborhood (Hongdae station, line 2). Held during the last two weeks of August, the festival presents hundreds of shows, exhibits, spontaneous concerts, films and street theater performances. www.seoulfringefestival.net/.

Seoul Oriental Medicine Festival

More and more people are exploring Oriental herbal medicine, and this festival, held at the Gyeongdong Herbal Medicine Market in eastern Seoul, is a great way to get up to speed on ancient Eastern remedies. Soak up the history and practices involved in centuries-old tonics or get some advice on curing what ails you.

Simply wandering the labyrinth of cubbyhole shops and vendors hawking exotic herbs, shrubs, and roots is loads of fun – and a break

Did you know...

that Seoul hosts the annual "e-stars Seoul" computer gaming tournament? In 2009, 118 teams from 14 countries engaged in virtual combat at the Seoul Trade and Exhibition Center (SETEC). Warcraft 3 and Counter-Strike 1.6 were the most popular games.

TAKE 5 FIVE TRADITIONAL
DANCES

1. *Geommu* (sword dance)

Geommu has been depicted on ancient frescoes dating to the Three Kingdoms period, and was later performed before the royal court and government officials of the Joseon Kingdom. The dance is military in origin, but is performed by women wearing beautiful, boldly colored costumes. Each performer holds a sword and dances using quick, expansive movements. A significant aspect of *geommu* involves the dancers turning around as they bend back and forth at the waist.

2. *Ganggangsullae* (circle dance)

Ganggangsullae is a women's circle dance performed during Chuseok, the Harvest Moon Festival celebrated in fall. One woman stands in the middle and sings solo, while those surrounding her voice the refrain. A theory about the dance's origin holds that it began in the sixteenth century when invaders menaced Korea. Korean women would dance in circles around fires to bolster the impression that the territory was well defended.

3. *Bongsan talchum* (mask dance)

Bongsan talchum is performed in spring and was originally intended as a ritual to drive away evil spirits. Later, it evolved into a more festive folk dance. *Bongsan Talchum* is a humorous dance that employs a cast of characters including a dissolute Buddhist priest, a degenerate aristocrat, a clever servant and an untrustworthy shaman. The mask dance draws on shamanism, Buddhism and other traditions to satirize the social order.

4. *Salpuri* (exorcism dance)

Salpuri was at one time performed by shamans to appease the spirits of the dead and allow the deceased to get to heaven. In the early twentieth century, *Salpuri* was adapted into a stage dance and performed with a white scarf as a prop. In Korea, the color white is sometimes associated with mourning and death.

5. *Buchaechum*

Buchaechum is a colorful neo-traditional Korean dance first choreographed in 1954 by Kim Baek-bong. *Buchaechum* features brilliant costumes, large and gorgeously decorated fans and upbeat music. The female dancers use the fans to make wavy patterns echoing flowers, butterflies and other aspects of the natural world.

from Seoul's modern face. The market is located near Jegi-dong station on line 1. Visit www.kyungdongmart.com (Korean only) or Seoul City Tourism at www.visitseoul.net for dates.

Hae Bang Chon (HBC) Music Festival

The twice-yearly Hae Bang Chon Fest takes place in May and October. Produced by Canadian musician and impresario Lance Reegan-Diehl, HBC is a guitar-heavy rock festival popular with ex-pats. It is held at a half-dozen venues in the Yongsan area and showcases scores of acts.www.hbcfest.com

TRADITIONAL MUSIC

Korean traditional music comes in many forms, from court music performed at elaborate ceremonies, to folk tunes played by rural peasants. The following are a few genres and styles.

Sanjo

Literally meaning "scattered melodies," *sanjo* is played solo and is an extremely challenging musical form. *Sanjo* can be played on various instruments including the *geomungo* (six-stringed zither), *gayageum* (twelve-stringed zither) and *daegeum* (long transverse bamboo flute). *Sanjo* starts slowly and then moves to a faster tempo, and is flexible enough to allow for improvisation. *Sanjo* requires precise technique and unusual musicality, and is often used to measure a performer's talent.

Jongmyo *jeryeak*

The tablets of ancient kings and queens are kept at Seoul's Jongmyo Shrine. Jongmyo *jeryeak* refers to the music, dance and song that are integral to the royal memorial rituals celebrated at Jongmyo. The music dates to the time of King Sejong (1418-1450), and has been used in ritual ceremonies since 1463. The South Korean government named Jongmyo *jeryeak* as Important Intangible Cultural Property No. 1, and UNESCO has placed Jongmyo Shrine on its World Heritage list as one of 689 cultural properties worldwide designated as having "outstanding universal value."

Pansori

Pansori is sometimes known as Korean folk opera, and consists of long narrative stories sung by a solo performer. *Pansori* incorporates *aniri* (narration), *sori* (singing), and *ballim* (acting). The singing is accompanied by drumming, and the percussionist encourages the singer throughout the performance with verbal interjections. *Pansori* dates to ancient times and was written down and refined in the eighteenth century; it was most popular during the nineteenth and early twentieth centuries. As *pansori* can take as long as eight hours to perform in its entirety, the form is now typically presented in abbreviated one or two-hour versions.

Minyo

Minyo are folk songs combining indigenous melodies and basic texts. *Minyo* vary regionally, and are generally divided into five styles hailing from different areas of the Korean Peninsula. Each region's *minyo* possesses a distinct mood and musical style. The songs from Jeju Island are the most abundant and number approximately 1,600.

Samulnori

Samul means "four objects," and *samulnori* refers to a percussion quartet consisting of *buk* (barrel drum), *janggu* (hourglass-shaped drum), *jing* (gong), and *kkwaenggwari* (small gong). The rhythmic patterns come from traditional rural and shamanistic music that was performed outdoors with acrobatic and dance movements. The principle of the music is the alternation of tension and relaxation. The percussionists improvise rhythms based on several patterns while attempting to achieve a perfect integration of the four instruments.

NATIONAL THEATER OF KOREA

The fabled National Theater of Korea (NTK) is home to the National Drama Company, the National *Changgeuk* (Korean musical drama) Company, the National Dance Company and the National Orchestra.

TAKE 5 RICHARD CHOI'S FIVE LEADING
DANCE CLUBS AND HIGH-END NIGHTSPOTS

Richard Choi is a founding partner of Nodus, a Seoul-based consulting and events production company. Nodus hosts regular upscale parties including First Thursdays Afterwork, a champagne party for young professionals to decompress and mingle with like-minded others, and Zodiac Lounge & Club, a premiere lounge and fine clubbing party. For more information about the party and events scene in Seoul, visit www.theNodus.com.

1. Club Volume (Crown Hotel)
An intense sound system and hypnotic light show have put this Itaewon club at number 29 on DJmag's list of the top 100 clubs worldwide. www.clubvolume.com.

2 .Eden (Ritz Carlton Hotel)
Located in the basement of one of Seoul's posh hotels, Eden is the go-to club in Gangnam. It consistently attracts some of the world's top DJs, and its resident disc spinners are hailed as some of Korea's best. The bar staff is hospitable, and the prices reasonable. www.eden-club.co.kr.

3. Heaven (Renaissance Hotel)
This recently opened club boasts a massive space and two distinct sound systems; it's a current favorite among Korean clubbers. www.clubheaven.co.kr.

4. Coffee Bar K in Cheongdam-dong.
A quiet and luxurious bar whose resident mixologist is ranked No. 1 in Korea, and No. 4 in the world, as of summer 2009. Sample out-of-this-world drinks, but be prepared to pay three times the cost of a typical meal for just one of these liquid treats.

5. Lound and "74."
These exclusive lounge bars are located next to each other in Cheongdam-dong, and offer an extensive list of cocktails. Sure, you will be paying 20,000 won for a drink, but everything about these places exudes quality. These establishments are on par with the famous Woobar, located in the W Hotel in eastern Seoul. Woobar often pops up in movies, typically in scenes where villains are seen popping bottles of Cristal.

The National Orchestra specializes in Korean traditional music.

The NTK dates to 1950 and is located at the base of Namsan Mountain. It is open year-round, and is a favored venue for traditional and contemporary performances of music, dance and drama. In addition to the 1,583-seat Main Hall, the NTK features a small hall, a studio, a youth theater and a cultural plaza. www.ntok.go.kr/english/index.do

WESTERN CLASSICAL MUSIC

Seoulites are classical music devotees, and the city has produced many well-known musicians. Some play locally, others are members of symphony orchestras worldwide.

The Seoul Philharmonic Orchestra (SPO) was founded in 1948 and reformed in 2005 under the direction of Myung-Whun Chung. The orchestra performed a Beethoven cycle in 2006, a Brahms series in 2007 and a Masterpiece series in 2008. Chung, who debuted at the SPO as a seven-year-old piano player, has served as the leader of orchestras in Germany, France, and Italy. In addition to Chung, the SPO (www.seoulphil.or.kr) is also home to the acclaimed Unsuk Chin, Korea's first composer-in-residence.

The SPO's home-grown talent has been augmented by distinguished visiting performers including violinist Leonidas Kavakos, cellist Jian Wang, and pianist Nicholas Angelich. The SPO has also welcomed such guest conductors as Charles Dutoit, James Judd, Mikko Franck, Andrey Boreyko and Pinchas Zukerman. The Seoul Philharmonic plays at the Sejong Center, as well as at the Seoul Arts Center and the LG Arts Center.

The KBS Symphony Orchestra and the Euro-Asian Philharmonic Orchestra are two other prominent Seoul orchestras. The latter was formed in the late 1990s, and specializes in Beethoven performances under the direction of Nanse Gum at the Seoul Arts Center.

The KBS Orchestra (http://kbsso.kbs.co.kr/eng/main.php) is the flagship orchestra of the Korean Broadcasting System. It performs at

KBS Hall and the Seoul Arts Center under the direction of Dmitry Kitaenko. In 1995, as part of the United Nations' 50th anniversary celebrations, the KBS Orchestra performed at the UN General Assembly Hall. In 2000, the orchestra made history when it gave four joint concerts with the North Korean State Symphony Orchestra.

TAKE5 FIVE LEADING ROCK VENUES

Korea has had a rock scene for several decades, although until the last 15 or so years it was largely underground. Korean rockers are no longer hiding, but they still have a tough time gaining recognition in a youth music landscape dominated by slickly produced and sugary sweet K-Pop confections. The university district of Hongdae is generally considered Seoul's best place to catch up-and-coming local rockers.

1. **Club Freebird.** A great all-around rock n' roll venue in Hongdae that features Korean and expat rock bands of all genres.

2. **Club FF.** Hongdae's best-known rock venue is located not far from Hongik University. There's always a crowd, and usually lots of foreigners.

3. **Badabie.** Located between Hongdae and Sinchon, this little basement venue features mostly experimental Korean bands performing to small audiences.

4. **Club Spot.** Near Hongik University, Spot is the go-to place for Korean punk and hardcore bands.

5. **Ye Olde Stompers Rock Spot.** Itaewon's best-kept secret for live music. Tucked away on top of the hill, this venue is where the expat locals head for stiff drinks and good music.

NANTA

Nanta blends comedy, Broadway glitz and traditional Korean rhythms. It's a fast-paced and entertaining musical popular with audiences of all ages and backgrounds.

Nanta starts with a simple premise: A team of chefs must create an elaborate wedding meal on short notice. The comic, non-verbal percussion performance takes this basic thread and weaves it in all kinds

TAKE5 MARK RUSSELL'S FIVE
KOREAN FILM CLASSICS

Mark Russell is a writer, producer and journalist who lived in South Korea for 13 years, writing for such publications as *The New York Times, Newsweek, Hollywood Reporter* and *Billboard*. In 2009, he published *Pop Goes Korea: Behind the Revolution in Movies, Music, and Internet Culture* (Stone Bridge Press), the first English-language book about the Korean Wave and Korea's culture and entertainment industry. He currently lives in Spain.

1. *The Host* (괴물) 2006. Directed by Bong Joon-ho. The highest-grossing movie in Korean film history stars the Han River (and a creature arising out of it). Exciting, audacious and ambitious in a way too few filmmakers attempt.

2. *Youngja on the Loose*, aka *Youngja's Heydays* (영자의 전성 시 대) 1975. Directed by Kim Ho-seon. This wild and crazy story about a lower-class woman's struggle for survival in the big city features lots of bad behavior and melodrama. There are also plenty of great views of 1970s Seoul, including the City Hall/Deoksu Palace area, and Yeouido when it was just starting to be developed.

of clever ways. The show has been a hit in Korea and abroad since its 1997 debut, and there are plenty of laughs as the goofy cooks chop and bang their way to their goal.

Along with the funny antics, there is some serious drumming as the performers employ knives, pots, pans and water bottles—basically whatever they can get their hands on—for use as percussive instruments. www.nanta.co.kr.

3. *Virgin Stripped Bare by Her Bachelors*, aka *Oh! Soo-jung!* (오! 수정) **2000.** Directed by Hong Sang-soo. Hong's best film is shot in beautiful black-and-white with a delicate but thoughtful sensibility. Most of this comedy drama (about a difficult romance involving a couple drawn from the film and gallery worlds) is set in the Insadong area. You can have endless fun tracking down and trying out the restaurants featured in the movie.

4. *Barefooted Youth* (맨발의 청춘) **1964.** Directed by Kim Ki-duk. One of the great films from Korea's golden age stars Shin Sung-il and Eom Aeng-ran at their best. A good-hearted lower-class thug develops a doomed relationship with a diplomat's daughter. Lots of style and pizzazz, plus plenty of great shots of a very different Seoul from the early 1960s.

5. *Green Fish* (초록 물고기) **1997.** Directed by Lee Chang-dong. Set just outside of Seoul, Green Fish is one of Lee's strongest films. Unable to find work in the developing edges of Seoul where he is from, the protagonist Makdong ends up getting involved with organized crime. The views of apartment buildings going up are full of ominous implications, but also form an interesting backdrop to the story, almost like an uncredited extra.

They said it

K-POP

Walk around Seoul, and sooner or later you'll hear K-pop (Korean pop music) blaring from an ice cream shop or seeping from a teenager's earbuds.

K-pop bands are usually manufactured. Prospective members audition, and if chosen, are then trained by a music company to sing and dance in unison. The telegenic ensembles typically perform either hip-hop-influenced dance music, or R&B-inspired ballads (known locally as *bal-la-deu*). The groups are popular throughout Asia, and some are even making waves in North America.

There are so many boy and girl bands vying for attention it's difficult to keep them straight, especially when they can be as large as the 13-member Super Junior (allegedly the world's largest boy band). In addition to the ensembles, established solo acts like BoA, Rain and Lee Hyori round out the pop scene.

Korean contemporary pop music is interesting in the way that *noraebang* (singing rooms) influence music writing and production. Visiting a *noraebang* and belting out songs made famous by the top stars of the day is a popular pastime in Korea. Consequently, many K-pop tunes are easy to sing, even for the modestly talented. Similarly, K-pop videos try to showcase something that fans can imitate, the goal being to start a popular dance craze rather than demonstrate moves requiring great skill.

BIG *BANG*

"*Bang*" is the Korean word for room, and Seoul's entertainment landscape includes a multitude of *bang* offering a wealth of diversions.

Noraebang (singing room)

Most people love to sing; they just hate the idea of doing so in front of strangers. The *noraebang* is similar to karaoke, but features private rooms outfitted with strobe lights, microphones, TVs and a large selection of songs (English, Korean, Chinese and Japanese titles are usually available). Some of the nicer *noraebang* even offer lofts, swings, flat-screen TVs and costumes. The *noraebang* is a popular post-dinner and drinks activity for groups.

DVD *bang* (DVD viewing room)

Customers choose and watch a movie in their own private room, which is typically outfitted with a large flat-screen TV, stereo system and couch. It's an easy "getaway" date for young couples.

Screen golf *bang* (golf simulation room)

The rooms are perfect for a late-night round of golf and come outfitted with clubs, balls and tees. Customers can "play" a full 18-holes, or simulate a driving range. There are a variety of courses to choose from, including some of the world's most famous. The best part is that you don't have to chase after lost balls.

Jjimjilbang

Jjimjilbang are basically large saunas where people go to sweat and relax. They are popular places to spend time with friends and family. Many of the bigger establishments have exercise equipment, computers, televisions, and even restaurants (all in heated rooms). *Jjimjilbang* also provide inexpensive accommodations for those traveling light. In some, you sleep on a mat on the floor, while others have bunk beds.

Jjimjilbang trace their origins to the bathhouses of yesteryear. The first bathhouse in Seoul was introduced in 1925 and was considered a luxury. As time passed, bathhouses became more popular, especially since most homes did not have their own bathing facilities. Despite the current ubiquity of modern indoor plumbing, there are thousands of saunas and *jjimjilbang* across Seoul. An estimated 150,000 tourists yearly visit one of these establishments while in Korea.

They said it

PC-*bang* (Internet cafe)

These rooms' lightning-fast computers make them particularly popular with young men who meet there to play online video games with their friends.

Manhwabang (comic book room)

Korean comics and graphic novels are called *manhwa*, and *manhwabang* are places where young people can hang out and read, trade and borrow comics.

ART MUSEUMS

Seoul has made a conscious decision to increase the quantity, and quality of its art museums and galleries. The buildings are world-class,

Did you know. . .

that one of South Korea's most popular TV shows is called *Misuda: A Chat With Beauties?* It features a panel of foreign women living in Korea talking about their experiences. The highly rated show debuted in 2006 and has featured women from a variety of nations including Uzbekistan, Germany, Italy, Kenya, Russia, Australia and Japan.

and the collections no less so. (For history museums, including several housing Korean cultural artifacts, folk art and traditional crafts, see the list "Five Major History and Culture Museums" in the "Then and Now" chapter).

Hallyu

Hallyu is the word for the now famous "wave" of Korean pop culture. The wave crested in the early 2000s when the Korean television dramas *Autumn Fairy Tale* (2000), *Winter Sonata* (2002), *Daejanggum* (2003) and *Full House* (2004) became wildly popular outside Korea. A number of Korean movie stars and music groups also caught on abroad, sparking a wider interest in Korean fashion, food and language.

The drama *Winter Sonata* is emblematic of *hallyu*. The program's star, Bae Yong-Joon, became a heartthrob in Japan, and Japanese tourists still come to Korea to visit the locations where the love story was filmed. Mr. Bae's allure has apparently even prompted some Japanese women to learn Korean!

Another product of the Korean Wave is Rain, whose real name is Jung Ji-Hoon. A pop star who crossed over to a successful career in television dramas and film, Rain parlayed this success into a career as an entertainment producer and business mogul. On the female side, Lee Young-Ae, star of the drama *Daejanggum*, is one of Korea's top models and spokespersons, and is hugely popular abroad.

The initial wave appeared to subside around 2005; the market apparently became saturated when too many entertainment companies tried to turn a quick buck by banking on the sudden enthusiasm for things Korean. A second surge has emerged, however, led by dance-pop groups like Super Junior, the Wonder Girls and Girls' Generation. The 2008 TV drama *Boys Before Flowers* was also a huge Korean and international hit.

Hallyu, which had its roots in the 1990s, is no longer a novelty and foreign demand for Korean pop culture remains high.

Seoul Museum of Art. Also known as SeMA, the Seoul Museum of Art is one of the city's most delightful museums, and a bargain to boot. It is housed in the old Supreme Court building and located in the heart of the city near Deoksugung Palace and City Hall. Past exhibitions have featured the works of such masters as Van Gogh, Picasso, Monet and Magritte. SeMA also exhibits contemporary artists, both Korean

TAKE5 FIVE POPULAR KOREAN TV DRAMAS

Korean dramas usually comprise 20 to 25 episodes and the story line is resolved at series' end. These melodramatic tales of love, family, war and business were extremely popular in the early 1990s, and still attract large audiences today. www.MySoju.com is a convenient gateway to find these programs and provides English subtitles. The following five dramas rank highly on MySoju's "Top 10 Dramas of All Time" list.

1. *Boys Over Flowers* **(2008).** Geum Jan-di is the daughter of a poor family who gets admitted into the ultra-elite Sinhwa High School after preventing a student's suicide attempt. She is ostracized by the rich students and bullied by a group of four popular boys. Jan-di refuses to be intimidated, and her stubborn determination wins over the boys. Eventually, she becomes enmeshed in a love triangle with two of them, and there are a series of complications involving family, memory loss and various real and feigned romances.

2. *The 1st Shop of Coffee Prince* **(2007).** Go Eun-chan is a tough, hardworking girl who works many side jobs to help support her family. She is so tough, in fact, that most people mistake her for a boy. This includes Choe Han-gyeol, the rich heir to a coffee empire, who decides to hire Eun-chan as his gay lover to avoid getting married. Over time, Han-gyeol finds himself falling for Eun-chan (whom he thinks is a boy), and he starts to question his own sexuality.

and international, and offers educational programs.

In addition to the main museum, SeMA has an annex in an elegant building in southern Seoul once occupied by the Belgian Embassy. Finally, there is also SeMA Gyeonghuigung, which is located in a renovated historic building at Gyeonghuigung Palace. http://seoul-moa.seoul.go.kr/global/eindex.jsp

3. *East of Eden* (2008). This 56-episode story about fate questions the importance of blood ties. As a teenager, Lee Dong-cheol witnessed his father's murder at the hands of Shin Tae-hwan. Lee spends his life seeking revenge against the murderer, and enlists the aid of his younger brother, Dong-uk, who has become a prosecutor. Later, it is revealed that Dong-uk was switched at birth with Shin's son, making Lee's brother and ally the murderer's son.

4. *We Got Married* (2008, 2009). A romantic "reality show" in which four couples are supposed to live a married life on TV. The couples are placed in uncomfortable scenarios to test their commitment to each other (and the show). As couples become less popular, they are often booted off the program.

5. *Shining Inheritance* (2009). It's a modern-day Cinderella story where a rich girl's father dies and her evil stepmother tries to steal her inheritance. The young girl, Go Eun-seong, works hard to become the chef of a famous food company. One day she meets Jang Suk-ja, an old woman suffering from amnesia who doesn't remember that she is the CEO of a famous company. Eun-seong takes care of the woman, and then later meets her grandson, the handsome but spoiled Seon Woo-hwan, who naturally falls in love with the plucky Eun-seong.

Leeum Samsung Museum of Art. The museum complex opened in 2004 and comprises three buildings designed by superstar architects Jean Nouvel, Mario Botta and Rem Koolhaas. Leeum Samsung exhibits traditional Korean art as well as modern and contemporary works by Korean and international artists.

The collection represents a who's who of the twentieth century's most influential artists and sculptors including Josef Albers, Frank

Bio Worlds of Nam June Paik

To call Nam June Paik a Korean artist is to vastly understate his reach. In the 1960s he invented the field of video art, and went on to achieve global renown.

Paik was born in Seoul in 1932 and left Korea in 1950 with his family, moving to Hong Kong and then Japan. He graduated from the University of Tokyo in 1956 and headed for Germany. While in Germany, Paik pursued passions for philosophy and music composition, and began collaborating with experimental music legend John Cage.

In the early 1960s, Paik was a boundary-breaking composer and performance artist. His first solo art exhibition was in 1963, and it employed his signature motif: televisions. Paik placed the monitors in odd positions, and used magnets to scramble their images.

Paik moved to New York in 1964 and soon was producing daring pieces in collaboration with cellist Charlotte Moorman. Paik and Moorman's performances incorporated music, video and sometimes bizarre action. Among their most famous pieces was Paik's "Opera Sextronique," the performance of which led to Moorman's arrest for public nudity.

Paik's experimental installations and performance pieces challenge traditional conceptions of art. His use of television screens, devices typically associated with mass entertainment rather than high culture, is a key element in his exploration of the nature of art, and the relationship of people to technology. Paik was also interested in methods of involving viewers in the artistic experience, rather than relegating them

Stella, Mark Rothko, Willem de Kooning, Andy Warhol, Jeff Koons, Damien Hirst and Nam June Paik. The Leeum Samsung Museum is located in Yongsan near the Hangangjin subway station. The Samsung Foundation of Culture also supports two other important local art museums: the Ho-Am Art Museum (which lies 45 minutes south of Seoul in Yongin) and the Rodin Gallery in central Seoul. http://leeum. samsungfoundation.org/eng/main.asp

to being passive observers.

In 1970 Paik collaborated with Japanese video engineer Shuya Abe on the Paik-Abe video synthesizer, and throughout the 1970s he gained increasing renown as an artist, teacher and thinker. His multimedia installations were shown in museums and galleries around the world, and on January 1, 1984 he broadcast "Good Morning, Mr. Orwell," an international telecast featuring various musicians, public figures and experimental artists. Later that decade, in connection with the 1988 Seoul Olympics, Paik created the tower-like "The More the Better," composed of over 1,000 video screens and standing 18 meters (59 feet) tall.

Paik continued to innovate throughout his career, and in the 1990s he used lasers in his installations. In recognition of his body of work, New York's Guggenheim Museum staged a career retrospective in 2000 entitled "The Worlds of Nam June Paik," an exhibit which was also mounted in Seoul.

Paik was a global artist who belonged to Korea, Germany, the U.S. and ultimately, the world. He died in 2006 in Miami. He left a tremendous artistic legacy in his use of new technologies, and in his mixing of artistic forms and genres. Paik's work remains profound and puzzling, arresting and humorous.

In 2008, the Nam June Paik Art Center opened in Yongin, 45 minutes south of Seoul. www.njp.kr.

TAKE 5 FIVE *MANHWA* OF INTEREST

Korean comics and graphic novels (*manhwa*) tend to be short and squat like their Japanese counterparts. Thousands of *manhwa* titles are published every year, and while many are essentially teen melodramas, there are some titles with wider appeal.

1. ***Kingdom of the Winds* by Kim Jin.** NETCOMICS, 2008, 216 pages paperback. Set in the ancient kingdom of Goguryeo, the story blends fact and fantasy in the tale of a cursed royal family led by an ambitious, vindictive king. Tragedy, warfare, romance and the spirit world all come into play in this epic tale. The book was made into a 36-episode television drama which aired in 2008-2009.

2. ***The Great Catsby* by Doha.** NETCOMICS, 2006. A comic multi-volume series about an unemployed recent college grad's attempts to get his life together after his girlfriend leaves him. The title is a play on the F. Scott Fitzgerald novel, and the series an astute portrayal of tortured youth, Korean style.

3. ***Eat Away: A Guide to the Heartland of Korean Cooking* by Young-Mahn Hur.** Gimm-Young Publishers, 2003. Stories about Korean food, cooking and culture by one of Korea's veteran *manhwa* artists and writers.

4. ***Korea Unmasked: In Search of the Country, the Society and the People* by Won-bok Rhie.** Gimm-Young International 2005, 236 pages, paperback. A well-known local cartoonist's account of the ideology and history of the Korean people. The book explains cultural differences between Korea, Japan and China, the Korean obsession with education, and even such topics as why Koreans typically don't apologize if they bump into you on the street.

5. ***Manhwa 100: The New Era for Korean Comics.*** NETCOMICS 2008, 248 pages, paperback. Published in connection with an exhibition at the Korean Cultural Centre in London, England celebrating 100 years of Korean comics, this guide summarizes the most popular *manhwa* titles.

National Museum of Contemporary Art. Located in Seoul Grand Park, the spacious three-floor museum has extensive grounds and features an outstanding outdoor sculpture garden. The museum has a large collection of Korean modern and contemporary art, as well as works by foreign artists. Nam June Paik's towering video installation "The More the Better" comprising 1,003 television monitors stands at the museum's center. www.moca.go.kr.

Deoksugung Palace Art Museum. This annex of the National Museum of Contemporary Art is in the west wing of Seokjojeon in Deoksugung Palace. It was built in 1938, and was Korea's first modern art exhibition space. It is an excellent place to sample contemporary art in central Seoul. www.moca.go.kr.

Bukchon Art Museum. Bukchon, which means "North Village," is located between Gyeongbokgung and Changdeokgung palaces, and features a mix of old and new art from China and Korea. The museum is also home to over 2,500 Joseon-era documents. www.bukchonartmuseum.com.

Seoul National University Museum of Art. SNU's museum opened in 2005 and is dedicated to modern and contemporary art. The Rem Koolhaas-designed building, which is dug into a hillside and appears to be a floating wedge, is worth the trip alone. www.snumoa.org.

Did you know. . .

that Korea is a leading center for subcontracted animation work? Much of the animation on *The Simpsons* (as well as that performed on other animated American television shows and movies) is done in Seoul. The trend started in the mid-1980s when Seoul's Akom Productions provided the animation for the first *My Little Pony* movie.

Hangaram Art Museum. This three-story museum is located in the Seoul Arts Center (SAC), a modern complex near the Nambu Bus Terminal. In addition to the Hangaram Art Museum, the SAC complex also contains the Hangaram Design Museum, the Seoul Calligraphy Art Museum, Opera House and Seoul Music House. www.sac.or.kr.

aA Design Museum. aA's space is stylish, open, contemporary and very hip. Located in the Hongdae area in Mapo, aA features four floors of industrial art, architecture and furniture from international designers including Tom Dixon and Pierre Paulin. www.aadesignmuseum.com.

LOTTE WORLD

Lotte World is Seoul's answer to Disney and the theme park's mascots, the effervescent squirrels Lotty and Lorry, wouldn't be out of place in Orlando or Anaheim. The Lotte World complex is in Jamsil in southern Seoul; it's a city within a city and attracts millions of visitors annually.

Lotte World features an indoor theme park (the world's largest), an outdoor theme and amusement park, a shopping mall, a department store, a discount/outlet store and a 533-room hotel. There is also an ice skating rink and other sports facilities, and, for the culturally inclined, the Lotte World Folk Museum. www.lotteworld.com.

SEOUL GRAND PARK AND SEOUL LAND

Seoul Grand Park is home to the world's tenth-largest zoo, and houses some 3,400 animals. In addition to the main zoo, there is a kids' zoo where youngsters can get up close with the animals, a zoological garden, a botanical garden (Asia's second-largest) and a rose garden with over 20,000 plants.

Seoul Grand Park is extensive and includes walking trails and a lake. Visitors can use the park's tram to get around, or ride the gondola (which provides great views). http://grandpark.seoul.go.kr/Eng/html/main/main.jsp.

Take Me Out to the Ball Game

Baseball Korean-style offers all the classic pleasures of the grand old game, but with a few delightful local twists. On the field, the game is nearly identical to its North American counterpart. What's different are some of the ballpark snacks (substitute dried squid for peanuts) and the cheerleaders.

Baseball was introduced to Korea by American missionaries in 1905, and in 1982 a professional league, the Korea Baseball Organization (KBO), was formed. Each team plays a 133-game schedule and is allowed two foreigners, typically former big-league players from the U.S. Three of the league's eight teams play in Seoul: the Doosan Bears, LG Twins and Seoul Heroes. Team names typically reflect the squad's corporate owner or sponsor, and so a match might pit the Kia Tigers against the Samsung Lions.

The KBO's young, energetic female cheerleaders wouldn't be out of place at an American pro football or basketball game. They are accompanied, however, by a cheering drill sergeant of sorts: a white-gloved man who races the length of the home team's dugout exhorting the fans. The cheer master uses a whistle and hand motions to fire up the crowd in a series of ritualistic call-and-response cheers. These sessions happen routinely throughout the game, and the crowd can go home hoarse from shouting. They might also leave with their arms numb from banging thunder sticks together. These soft, inflated plastic tubes are a Korean invention, and went on to become popular at stadiums in North America.

There are foreign players in Korean baseball, but likewise several Korean players have cracked the big leagues in the United States. Chan Ho Park, whose career began in 1994 with the Los Angeles Dodgers, is probably the best known. Korea has also fared well in international play. In 2008 the Korean squad won the gold medal at the Beijing Olympics, and in 2009 Korea finished second (to Japan) in the 16-team World Baseball Classic.

Located not far from the zoo is Seoul Land, an amusement/theme park comprising five areas: World Plaza, Adventure Land, Fantasy Land, Tomorrow Land and Samchulli (Folk) Land. Seoul Land has rides, performances and exhibits for kids of all ages; seasonal attractions include an outdoor pool and a sledding course. The skies light up on summer nights with fireworks and laser shows. http://eng.seoulland.co.kr/.

SPACE MAN

Designer and mogul Andre Kim is Korea's long-time man of fashion. The seventy-something couturier is an arresting presence himself: His head is painted a shiny black, and for several decades he has worn nothing but baggy white space suits in public. He changes the suits throughout the day, and told *The New York Times*: "There came a time when I could no longer wear tailored suits in a way that satisfied the style. The suit I designed is not only futuristic, it covers the figure I lost by not exercising."

Born in 1935 in a village outside Seoul, Kim rose to prominence in the early 1960s when he brought contemporary Western styles and color to a country struggling to recover from the effects of war. A prolific designer and dynamic businessman, Kim has mounted hundreds of fashion shows in Korea and abroad. Not only does he design clothes, his name has been attached to everything from housewares and appliances to golf gear and cosmetics.

Kim's diverse design commissions have included everything from the South Korean athletes' uniforms for the 1988 Seoul Olympics to Miss Universe Pageant dresses. In 1997 he was awarded a Presidential Culture and Art Medal, and has also received a number of other domestic and foreign honors. Despite this acclaim, the flamboyant Kim remains a man of the people. He was once approached by Michael Jackson and asked to serve as the gloved one's personal designer; Kim declined on the grounds that his clothes were for "everyone."

LUCKY SEVEN

Visitors to Seoul hankering for a bit of gaming excitement are in luck! Seven Luck Casino operates two full-fledged casinos in the city, one on each side of the river. Both are open 24 hours and conveniently located amidst the luxury hotels belt.

North of the river, head to the Millennium Seoul Hilton on Namsan; south of the river, the Gangnam branch is attached to the Oakwood Premiere, just a chip's throw from the COEX mall. The Seven Luck casinos are open to foreigners only (passport ID required), and games include baccarat, Tai Sai (a Chinese dice game), Caribbean stud poker, three-card poker, blackjack, and the house game, Seven Luck 21. It pays to familiarize yourself with the local table rules in Seoul, which can differ from those elsewhere. In the local version of blackjack, the dealer must take cards until showing 17, and insurance is offered when he shows an ace. Black jack tables at Seven Luck offer minimum bets as low as 2,000 won (about two U.S. dollars). Those with a little more cash to throw around can hit the high-end tables, which max out at five million won (four to five thousand U.S. dollars) per bet. For those who don't want to mix it up at the tables, there are also slot machines, including video poker.

Chinese, Japanese and overseas Korean and Western businessmen account for the lion's share of gamblers, who are served free cocktails, beer, and coffee at their tables by waitresses. Dealers can speak a bit of English and Japanese, but dice, cards and blinking slots serve as the universal language. Before entering, sign up for a Seven Luck membership card, which will accumulate "points" as you play and award you meals and other perks in the accompanying restaurants and lounges.

The blackjack and roulette tables attract a loyal following and can get crowded, so visit during off-hours or on weekdays if you prefer some breathing room. This might be Seoul, but the clamor of players' shouts, whoops and cries—often in Chinese—gives Seven Luck an international flair – Macao crossed with Vegas, kissed with a Korean touch.

THE SPORTING LIFE

Seoul offers great opportunities for the athlete and sports enthusiast. Hiking is popular in the mountains in and around Seoul, and the banks of the Han River are outstanding for jogging, biking and inline skating. Other choice locations to get the blood circulating include World Cup Park, Olympic Park and Seoul Forest.

Seoul also has many skating rinks, swimming pools, bowling alleys and fitness centers. For armchair enthusiasts, there are plenty of professional and amateur sporting events. Soccer fans will want to take in the World Cup Museum at World Cup Park, and Olympic diehards can visit the Olympic Museum at Olympic Park.

Soccer Mania

Koreans love soccer, and they were richly rewarded for that devotion when the South Korean squad finished a strong fourth in the 2002 World Cup.

South Korea's professional soccer league was founded in 1983 and is known as the K-League. There are 15 member teams from around the nation, and the season runs from March until December. FC Seoul, which plays at Seoul World Cup Stadium, is Seoul's K-League representative. In addition to FC Seoul, there are three other teams based in the capital region: Incheon United, Suwon Samsung Bluewings and Seongnam Ilhwa Chunma.

Did you know. . .

that prior to hosting the 1988 Summer Olympics, Seoul hosted the 1986 Asian Games? Nearly 5,000 athletes from 22 nations participated, and the Republic of Korea finished second in the medal count after China. Seoul's neighbor to the west, the port city of Incheon, will serve as host of the 2014 Asian Games.

Taekwondo

Taekwondo, Korea's national sport, is a traditional martial art that uses the hands and feet. Like many martial arts, taekwondo's mental, spiritual and cultural aspects are just as important as flying feet and fists.

Taekwondo originated several millennia ago in tribal times, and during the Three Kingdoms period (57 BC to AD 668) was a part of military training. It later evolved into a popular folk practice or game.

Since the 1970s, taekwondo has taken on a global profile, and is now practiced by as many as 60 million people worldwide. Taekwondo served as a demonstration sport at the 1988 Seoul Olympics, and debuted as an Olympic medal event at the 2000 Sydney Games. For information on taekwondo demonstrations and exhibitions in Seoul, visit www.taekwonseoul.org.

High Wire Act

Every year, Seoul hosts the annual Han River High Wire World Championship, an event which typically attracts about 20 participants from countries around the world. A one-kilometer (0.6 mi.) wire is strung from one side of the Han to the other, and the competitors, using nothing more than a balancing pole and a lot of concentration, race across the single strand. The 2009 winner, Alfred Nock Junior of Switzerland, cleared the river in just over 10 minutes.

Did you know. . .

that Korea has a professional basketball league? The 10-team Korean Basketball League (KBL) began play in 1997, and has two Seoul-based squads. KBL players are primarily Korean-born with two imports allowed per team.

Golf

Koreans are fanatical golfers. There are many courses in the Seoul area, not to mention hundreds of indoor and outdoor practice ranges. Korean women are dominant players internationally and routinely place among the leaders in top tournaments. Jiyai Shin is one of the hottest players in women's golf today, and is following in the footsteps of World Golf Hall of Famer Se Ri Pak (one of the world's top female pros of the 1990s and 2000s) and Korean-American powerhouse Michelle Wie. And, on the male side, Y.E. Yang famously defeated Tiger Woods for the 2009 PGA Championship.

Marathon Men (and Women)

The Seoul International Marathon began in 1931 as the Dong-A Marathon. The course originally measured 50 *ri* (a traditional Chinese unit of measure), equivalent to about 14 kilometers or nine miles. It became a regulation marathon distance event in 1964.

Koreans are top marathoners and have achieved excellent results at the Olympics (two gold medals), as well as winning such premier events as the Boston Marathon. The Seoul International Marathon, which takes place in March, attracts around 10,000 entrants. The course begins at Gwanghwamun Square in downtown Seoul, and ends at Olympic Stadium in Jamsil.

In addition to the Seoul International Marathon, there is the upstart JoongAng Seoul Marathon which debuted in 1999 and is held in the fall. The race begins and ends at Olympic Stadium and attracts more than 20,000 entrants. It is a wonderful event for enjoying the autumn foliage. JoongAng is not just for seasoned marathoners – it includes a companion 10 kilometer (6 mile) race for runners who want to get a taste of the marathon experience, while not going too hard on their legs, knees and lungs.

Weblinks

GOVERNMENT SPONSORED SITES

Seoul City Tourism

www.visitseoul.net

Managed by the Seoul Metropolitan Government, the site has plentiful information on festivals, activities, museums and sights along the themes of traditional, modern and outdoor Seoul. There are also links to many other sites. Call DASAN Seoul call center 120(9) from Seoul.

Seoul Convention Bureau

www.miceseoul.com/

Of particular interest to meeting planners and tourism professionals.

Seoul Metropolitan Government

www.seoul.go.kr

An in-depth site listing events, activities and attractions of all kinds for tourists, businesspeople and locals.

Korea Tourism Organization (KTO)

www.visitkorea.or.kr

Seoul naturally figures heavily in the wide-ranging KTO site. Click on "Seoul" under the "Destinations" heading.

Republic of Korea Official Website

www.korea.net

A lively site with material on Korean culture and other topics. Plenty of information on sights and events in Seoul and elsewhere.

NEWSPAPERS, MAGAZINES AND OTHER SITES OF INTEREST

Korea Times

www.koreatimes.co.kr

A local English-language daily with an extensive "weekend arts/culture" page.

JoongAng Daily

http://joongangdaily.joins.com/

An English language newspaper site that features "Foreign community" and "Culture" tabs in addition to domestic news.

Korea Herald

www.koreaherald.co.kr

Check out the "Culture" tab in what bills itself as "The Nation's No. 1 English Newspaper."

Chosun Ilbo

english.chosun.com

Check out the "Arts and Entertainment" and "Inside Korea" tabs in the English language edition of this major Seoul daily.

Koreana

www.koreana.or.kr

A quarterly on Korean arts and culture for international readers published by the Korea Foundation.

Seoul Selection/Seoul Magazine

www.seoulselection.com

Seoul Magazine and the on-line *Seoul Weekly* are published in cooperation with the Seoul Metropolitan Government. The site features plenty of leisure, tourism and entertainment information for expats and visitors. Seoul Selection also has an online bookshop featuring a wide array of English-language books on Seoul and Korea.

10 Magazine
www.10magazine.asia
Korea-wide coverage of nightlife, film, dining and arts and entertainment. Plenty of Seoul-related coverage, and a handy list of local English-language blogs.

Groove
www.seoulstyle.com
Arts, entertainment, dining and features aimed at expats.

Eloquence
www.eloquence.co.kr/eloquence/index.htm
"International Culture & Entertainment" covering sports, music and other areas.

Itaewononline/PR Magazine
www.itaewononline.com/
Specializing in nightlife, dining and shopping in the Itaewon neighborhood.

SITES TARGETING EXPATS

www.korea4expats.com
A comprehensive site focused on living and working in Korea which also has information on arts, culture, entertainment, clubs and social activities. Check out the bottom of the page for an excellent list of links to other sites.

Life in Korea
www.lifeinkorea.com
Click on the Information/Activities/Culture tab.

Economy

The Miracle on the Han—South Korea's transformation in a few short decades from impoverished country into the world's 13th largest economy—put Seoul on the map as a worldwide business capital. Today's high-tech metropolis was scarcely imaginable 60 years ago when many Seoulites did not have enough to eat. Following the Korean War, South Korea was poorer than North Korea, and it trailed the North in per capita income well into the 1960s (it is now light years ahead of its northern neighbor).

Since the 1950s, South Korea has moved from a largely agrarian nation to a leading producer of ships, motor vehicles, consumer goods and IT products. Anyone who drives a Hyundai or a Kia car, talks on a Samsung phone, or owns a Samsung or LG television, refrigerator, DVD player or air conditioner is familiar with South Korea's global economic reach. And how does all of that good stuff leave Korea? On Korean-built ships manufactured from, you guessed it, Korean-made steel.

As in most advanced economies, the service and information sectors are on the rise, and metropolitan Seoul stands at the forefront of South Korea's transition to a knowledge-based economy. Korea's IT industry is world class, and Seoul's recently developed Digital Media

They said it

City represents a major investment in this fast-growing sector.

Seoul's proximity to both China and Japan positions it ideally as a northeast Asian business hub. Korea is headquarters to 14 global Fortune 500 firms, 11 of which are based in Seoul. Moreover, more than half of the Fortune Global 500 maintain offices in Seoul, confirming the city's status as a leading player on the international business stage.

SOUTH KOREA BY THE NUMBERS

GDP: $1.343 trillion (2009).

GDP composition: services 58 percent; industry 39 percent; agriculture 3 percent.

GDP world ranking: 13 of 227 (between Spain and Canada).

Per capita GDP: $27,700.

Per capita GDP world ranking: 49 of 227 (between Slovenia and New Zealand).

Labor force: 24.4 million.

Labor force composition: services 68 percent; industry 25 percent; agriculture 7 percent.

Unemployment rate: 4.1 percent (2009).

Inflation: 2.8 percent (2009).

Exports: $355.1 billion (2009).

World rank as exporter: 8th (between Italy and the United Kingdom).

Imports: $313.4 billion (2009).

World rank as importer: 11th (between Belgium and Canada).

Currency: the Korean won (KRW) or ₩.

TAKE 5 TOP FIVE KOREAN COMPANIES
BY REVENUE

Revenues are in millions of dollars in 2008.
1. **Samsung Electronics** 110,350 (Seoul)
2. **LG** (electronics) 82,082 (Seoul)
3. **SK Holdings** (petroleum refining) 80,810 (Seoul)
4. **Hyundai Motor** 72,542 (Seoul)
5. **POSCO** (steel production) 37,976 (Pohang)

SEOUL

Seoul metropolitan region GDP: $408.6 billion.

Seoul metropolitan region GDP as a percentage of national GDP: 48.

City of Seoul income taxes: $3.09 billion (2004); 47 percent of national total.

City of Seoul corporate taxes: $13.52 billion (2004); 57 percent of national total.

City of Seoul bank deposits: 50 percent of national total (2005).

Number of businesses: 733,759.

Number of employees: 3,894,666.

Venture companies: 3,832 (2006); 31 percent of national total.

Sources: Seoul Metropolitan Government, Government of Korea, CIA World Factbook

DISPOSABLE INCOME

Seoul leads Korea in per capita disposable income. In 2008, Seoulites enjoyed 15.5 million won of yearly per capita disposable income. A close second to Seoul was Ulsan, home to Korea's shipbuilding industry, where residents averaged 15.35 million won in disposable income. Disposable income reflects income minus taxes and transfers; it does not take into account Seoul's high cost of living relative to the national average.

TAKE 5 YOUNG-IOB CHUNG'S FIVE
ASPECTS OF THE SOUTH KOREAN ECONOMY

Young-Iob Chung, Ph.D., is emeritus professor of economics at Eastern Michigan University. He was born in Korea, attended Seoul National University, and received his Ph.D. in economics from Columbia University. Dr. Chung has published two books on the Korean economy: *Korea Under Siege, 1876-1945* (Oxford University Press, 2006), and *South Korea in the Fast Lane* (Oxford University Press, 2007). He has also written dozens of academic articles, reviews, and conference papers on the Korean economy and other topics.

1. Four Stages in the Korean Economy's Development
In the past 135 years, the Korean economy has moved from an underdeveloped economy to an industrialized one. The transformation has occurred in four stages: 1) pre-1876 -- a completely closed traditional economy; 2) 1876 to 1910 -- an open yet traditional and agrarian economy; 3) 1910 to World War II -- a colonial economy under Japan; 4) World War II to present – a productive, independent free market economy in the Republic of Korea, and a parallel and wholly separate communist economy in North Korea.

2. The Rapidly Developing and Changing Economy
Out of the ashes of the catastrophic Korean War, and with the help of U.S. aid and foreign investment, South Korea has moved from a semi-industrial agrarian economy to a highly industrialized and developed one. Since the Korean War, South Korea has increased its GDP at an average annual rate of between five percent and eight percent. Until the latest global recession, the South Korean economy was one of the fastest growing in the world. At the end of the Korean War, agricultural production was about 40 percent of GDP and occupied roughly 60 percent of the labor force. The agricultural sector now produces less than a tenth of GDP, and employs only about two-tenths of the labor force.

3. A Highly Competitive Economy

Technologically, South Korea has striven for decades to catch up to the world's leading industrialized countries, particularly the U.S. and Japan. Now, South Korean companies have successfully penetrated world markets in a number of areas and are beginning to challenge for supremacy in some industrial fields, including high tech and automobiles.

4. A Hard-working and Educated Labor Force

Korean workers are hard-working and well educated. They realize that in order for Korea to be competitive with the world's advanced economies, they have to work extra hard and long to meet the challenge. Until very recently, Koreans' average working hours were some of the longest in the industrialized countries. Education is highly valued, and Korean universities are very competitive; moreover many of South Korea's business and political leaders have been educated abroad, particularly in the U.S.

5. The Key Role of International Trade

The South Korean economy is based largely on foreign trade (exports plus imports) which equals about 70 percent of GDP. The country imports oil, raw materials, and capital goods, while exporting various manufactured goods including automobiles, electronics, cell phones, and many other consumer goods.

SOUTH KOREAN PER CAPITA GROSS NATIONAL INCOME

1980	$2,600
1985	$4,530
1990	$8,200
1995	$12,770
2000	$17,050
2005	$22,760
2008	$28,120

THE MIGHTY *JAEBOL*

Jaebol are far-reaching business conglomerates that stretch across a number of industries. Due to their great size, they are vitally important to Korea's export-oriented economy. In the 1960s and 1970s, the *jaebol*'s close ties with government were vital in developing South Korea into a globally competitive nation. This bond has proved to be both blessing and curse, however, and the *jaebol* have been criticized for their undue influence on the government.

There have been several high-level corruption scandals involving *jaebol*, and as a result, reforms were initiated in 2000 that sought to limit their size and clout. Despite the grumbling about *jaebol*, nobody can deny their tremendous success, and brands like Samsung, Hyundai and LG are known to consumers the world over. Not surprisingly, jobs with these titans are highly prized among Koreans.

Did you know. . .

that a 2008 *Forbes* magazine survey ranked Seoul the world's ninth most economically powerful city? The Seoul urban agglomeration was also ranked as the planet's 21st largest in terms of GDP in 2008 (between Miami and Toronto).

MOTOR VEHICLE PRODUCTION

Korea produced 3.8 million vehicles in 2008, up from 3.1 million in 2000. Korea is ranked fifth worldwide in vehicle production, trailing only Japan, China, the U.S. and Germany. Hyundai-Kia ranks in the top five automakers worldwide.

The first car manufactured in Korea was the Sibal ("new beginning"), built by auto mechanic Choi Mu-seong and his brothers beginning in 1955. The Sibal resembled a U.S. Army Jeep and had a top speed of 80 kilometers per hour (50 mph). Three thousand Sibals (which were mostly used as taxis) were manufactured before production ended in 1963.

The Hyundai Motor Company was established in 1967 and became a significant auto manufacturer in the 1970s. In 2008, Hyundai produced 2.8 million vehicles worldwide. The Hyundai Tucson SUV is Korea's most-exported automobile. Between 2005 and 2009, nearly a million Tucsons were shipped abroad, primarily to Europe and South America.

Hyundai Motor is a truly global brand. It began selling cars in Africa in 1976 (moving 207 Pony vehicles that first year). In June 2009, the one millionth Hyundai was sold in Africa and Hyundai has the second-largest share of the African car market, trailing only Toyota.

IT

South Korea is an IT juggernaut, and as is the case with many Korean industries, its rise has been meteoric.

The Korean IT industry found its legs in 1981 when Sambo Engineering developed the first Korean computer. By the mid-1980s, South Korea was manufacturing and exporting large numbers of computers, topping the two million mark in 1989.

The Internet arrived in South Korea in 1995, and high-speed service debuted in 1998. A year later, Cyworld, the Korean social networking site, was inaugurated (beating MySpace and Facebook to the punch). By the mid-2000s, 85 percent of Korean households had at least one computer, and South Korea had established itself as one of the globe's premier IT nations.

TAKE 5 FIVE LEADING
JAEBOL

1. Samsung Group

The largest *jaebol* in Korea, Samsung (meaning "three stars"), was founded in 1938 by Lee Byung-chul and grew from a small factory employing 40 people to the largest conglomerate in Korea. Samsung is nearly the same size as Korea's second and third *jaebol* combined, and it represents 20 percent of Korean exports.

Samsung, arguably the most popular electronics brand in the world, is also a leading manufacturer of microchips and LCD panels, and the world's second-largest producer of cell phones. But electronics are not Samsung's only business: Samsung Heavy Industries is the world's second-largest shipbuilder, and Samsung C&T has played a key role in the construction of some of the world's tallest buildings including the Taipei 101 (Taiwan), Burj Khalifa (United Arab Emirates) and one of the Petronas Twin Towers (Malaysia).

2. Hyundai-Kia

Hyundai-Kia traces its roots to the Hyundai construction company which was established in the late 1940s. Hyundai, which means "modern," at first concentrated on simple building projects. Later, with the aid of the South Korean government, Hyundai expanded into cement production, shipbuilding, motor vehicles and even aeronautics.

In the 1980s and 1990s, and particularly after the 1997 Asian financial crisis, Hyundai was split up into a number of firms. Among these new companies was Hyundai Motor Company, which in 1998 purchased Kia Motors (Korea's second-largest automobile manufacturer) and formed Hyundai-Kia. This company is the largest automaker in Korea, and a major player worldwide.

3. SK

SK, formerly known as Sunkyung Group, began in 1953 as a textile company and soon expanded into the oil business as part of its "Petroleum to Fibers" strategy. SK has diversified into telecommunications, construction, hotels and entertainment, medical research, energy development and mining. Among other ventures, SK controls two luxury hotels in eastern Seoul, the Sheraton Grande Walkerhill and W Seoul. SK Telecom also has a more than 50 percent share of Korea's wireless market.

4. LG

LG (once known as "Goldstar" and later as "Lucky Goldstar") is Korea's fourth largest *jaebol*. In 1947 the Koo family founded Lak-hui (Lucky) Chemical and in 1952 it became Korea's first plastics manufacturer. The company also produced personal and household products, and was well known for its toothpaste. In 1967 LG entered into a joint venture with Caltex (Chevron and Texaco), and built one of the world's largest oil refineries in Yeosu, on the south coast. LG manufactured its first radio in 1959 and is a major brand worldwide in the area of cell phones, televisions, DVD players and appliances. LG operates subsidiaries in over 80 countries; its initials have morphed into the company's current slogan "Life's Good."

5. Lotte

Lotte was founded in 1948 in Tokyo by Korean businessman Shin Kyuk-ho. The company's name comes from a nickname for Charlotte, the heroine of a 1774 novel by the German writer Johann Wolfgang von Goethe.

Lotte began as a candy and gum company and soon expanded into the manufacture of food products. In 1967, following the resumption of diplomatic relations between South Korea and Japan, Lotte established companies in Seoul. In addition to the food and beverage industry, Lotte is also active in hotels, amusement parks, department stores, electronics, chemicals and financial services.

South Korea unites ultra-fast networks, superior IT technology, and a leading position as both a consumer and producer of computer products and cell phones. Korea has 37.5 million Internet users (10th in the world) and its Internet penetration rate is the highest among the OECD nations. South Korea is second (to the Netherlands) worldwide in its rate of broadband subscribers.

IT products represent one-third of Korean exports, and totaled $121 billion in 2009. The three anchors of the Korean IT industry are semiconductors (chips and transistors), display panels and mobile phones.

Samsung is the leader in Korea's IT field. It is one of the world's largest, if not the largest, manufacturer of DRAM chips, flash memory and optical storage devices. Samsung and LG are also leaders in the manufacture of liquid crystal display (LCD) and organic light emitting diode (OLED) screens, as well as plasma display panels. These products are found in electronic signs, cell phones, TVs, personal computers, e-book readers and laptops. Just like semiconductors, display panels and screens form the backbone of a range of information and entertainment devices and enable Korea's IT companies to establish their brand across many different products.

Samsung and LG are also leaders in the cell phone industry. As with computers, a strong domestic market provides a springboard for research and development and fuels foreign sales. South Korea has 45.6 million cell phones and cell phone usage is 93 percent. Logging on or placing a call is possible anywhere in Seoul, unlike in many places in North America where dropped calls and spotty network coverage remain a problem. Korea has a third of the worldwide cell phone market (shipping over 250 million cell phones) and Samsung and LG are the world's number two and three companies (after Nokia) in the field.

In order to bolster the development of digital content and promote

Did you know. . .

that according to the World Bank, South Korea ranks 19th out of 183 economies worldwide in terms of ease of doing business?

Bio Chung Ju-yung:
The Tycoon as Everyman

Hyundai Group founder Chung Ju-yung (1915-2001) remains Korea's most famous entrepreneur, and represents a true rice-to-riches story. The eldest of eight children, Chung was born in what is now North Korea. He spent his early days on the farm, but left home while still a teen. After working for short periods in construction and at a syrup factory, he landed a delivery position with a rice merchant. By 1937, Chung's hard work and initiative resulted in his owning the rice store; however, rice rationing forced him to close two years later.

Undaunted by this reversal, Chung turned to automobiles and ran a successful repair shop. He had nearly 70 employees, but again was forced to close because of World War II. Post-war, Chung opened another garage and also ran a construction company. When the Korean War broke out, he ferried supplies and built barracks for the U.S. Army. From these humble origins Hyundai became a leading international ship and motor vehicle manufacturer, and a global force in the construction and engineering field.

Chung, a fan of *ssireum* (Korean-style wrestling) who left school at 14, was driven, ambitious and blunt. He believed in hard work and simple living, and embodied the Miracle on the Han in which a poor nation became a rich one through diligence, determination and astute decision-making. Chung also took a keen interest in politics and made an unsuccessful 1992 bid for the Korean presidency.

Chung had a soft spot for his roots in the North, and worked relentlessly to help smooth relations between North and South Korea. His efforts included sending 1,001 cattle to North Korea, and arranging for tourist cruises to the Mount Geumgang region. Chung died in 2001 at age 85, his dream of a reunified Korea unfulfilled, but his legacy as an entrepreneur assured.

the IT industry, Seoul has developed the Digital Media City (DMC). The project takes in nearly 0.6 square kilometers (0.2 square miles) in western Seoul near World Cup Stadium and features multiple buildings, facilities and plazas. The DMC's digital media entertainment cluster is aimed at fostering innovation in the area of digital media content. It brings together media and technology companies, universities, R & D institutions and venture incubators. There is also an International Business Center and a "Digital Media Street" exposing consumers to the latest in domestic and foreign digital content.

TRADE

South Korea's 2009 exports totaled $355.1 billion. Major exports include semiconductors, wireless telecommunications equipment, motor vehicles, computers and display panels, steel, ships and petrochemicals. South Korean imports totaled $313.4 billion and were dominated by machinery, electronics and electronic equipment, oil, steel, transport equipment, organic chemicals and plastics.

MAJOR TRADING PARTNERS:

Percentage of Exports		Percentage of Imports	
China	21.4	China	17.7
U.S.	10.9	Japan	14.0
Japan	6.6	U.S.	8.9
Hong Kong	4.6	Saudi Arabia	7.8

Did you know...

that in the 1970s South Korea was known as one of the four "Asian Tigers"? South Korea was grouped with Hong Kong, Taiwan and Singapore as nations which in a short period of time underwent rapid industrialization and demonstrated strong export-oriented growth.

They said it

"Linked by high-speed broadband lines and blanketed by wireless signals capable of sending HDTV to tiny cell phones, South Korea is the world's most wired—and wireless—country."

– CNN in a 2008 "Eye on South Korea" story titled "More wired, less wire."

NORTH KOREA TRADE AND GDP

Unlike South Korea, one of the world's top trading nations, North Korea is a mostly closed economy. The dollar value of South Korea's exports is roughly 170 times that of its northern neighbor.

North Korea's total 2008 exports were estimated at $2.1 billion, although this figure may be lower than the real amount due to illicit sales of weapons and other prohibited goods. North Korea's chief exports include minerals, metallurgical products, weapons, textiles and agriculture and fisheries products. Forty-five percent of North Korean exports go to South Korea, 35 percent to China and five percent to India.

Total North Korean imports are estimated at 3.6 billion. The country's major imports are petroleum, coking coal, machinery and equipment, textiles and grain. Major sources of imported goods are China (46 percent of the total) and South Korea (34 percent).

North Korea's GDP per capita is estimated at $1,800 (2008), ranking it 188th out of 227 countries worldwide. On a per capita basis, the North's GDP is about 6.5 percent that of the South.

Did you know. . .

that the five-day workweek for office workers only became common in Korea in the early and mid-2000s? Previously, office workers, including those at banks and government offices, routinely worked on Saturdays. The change has represented a boost for the Korean leisure, tourism and hospitality industries.

CHARGE IT

In the late 1990s, the Korean government encouraged the use of credit cards and instructed businesses to become more credit-card friendly.

Unlike in North America where credit cards have been widespread since the 1970s, until 2000 credit cards were comparatively rare in Korea; consumers paid cash for most things. Credit card regulations were changed, however, and within a few years credit cards had become common. Soon, many consumers were in over their heads, as were the banks that had issued all that plastic. A meltdown occurred

1997 Economic Crisis

In the mid-1990s Korea's economy was booming: GDP was climbing steadily (as it had been since the 1960s), and Koreans were beginning to enjoy the consumer-oriented lifestyle long popular in the West.

By early 1997, however, there were warning signs that the Korean economy was in danger. In short, some of the big corporations and *jaebol* had over-extended themselves and were deeply in debt. Several filed bankruptcy, including Hanbo Steel and the Kia *jaebol*.

Korean banks were also in danger of insolvency, and some were unable to pay their foreign debts. The banks had speculated in the economies of several Asian nations, and when the Philippines, Thailand, and Indonesia began to falter and their currencies tumbled, the Korean economy was dragged down with them. The Korean won declined substantially in value, and the country was in the throes of an economic crisis.

On December 3, 1997, Korea agreed to accept $58 billion worth of aid from the International Monetary Fund (IMF). Part of the agreement was that Korea raise interest rates and open itself up to greater foreign investment. Within months the effects of the changes were being felt by the average Korean; unemployment rose to 1.8 million and the concept of lifetime employment was erased. Public payrolls were cut by 18 percent. Placards were seen in 2003 in the wake of widespread consumer defaults.

The situation has since vastly improved, and there has been a correction in both card issuance and spending habits. South Koreans possess 3.78 credit and debit cards per capita, more than the British (2.36), but fewer on average than Americans (5.3 cards). Credit cards are currently accepted in most places of business, even for the smallest amounts. Memory cards in cell phones are another form of credit; these can be used to pay public transportation fares and debited for small purchases.

in the streets declaring that IMF meant "I'M Fired."

Average Koreans rallied around their country. In a show of national unity, families donated their gold rings, watches, and necklaces in an effort to pay off Korea's foreign debt. Nearly $1.3 billion dollars worth of gold was collected and used to purchase foreign currency reserves. So much gold was collected that it drove the international gold price to its lowest level in more than 18 years.

Korea was one of the first Asian nations to recover from the economic collapse, but it had been costly. The powerful Daewoo Group went bankrupt, and of the 53 commercial and merchant banks operating in Korea in 1997, only 26 remained by 2001. Still, by early 1999 the major credit rating agencies had upgraded Korea's debt rating to "investment grade." Moreover, Korea paid off its IMF loan on August 23, 2001—three years ahead of schedule—and was the only country to do so in advance of its timetable.

Post-crisis, Korea returned to high economic growth, which did not let up until the beginning of the global recession. Certain negative aspects of the 1997 crisis do remain, including less employment security and a greater divide between the haves and have-nots. On the plus side, the crisis provoked a number of reforms in both the public and private sectors, many of which have had a beneficial effect on the Korean economy's long-term health.

SEOUL, A BARGAIN

A 2009 study by the financial firm UBS ranked 73 cities worldwide in terms of cost. Seoul was the 43rd most expensive, standing between Sao Paulo, Brazil, and Riga, Latvia. The five most expensive cities were Oslo, Zurich, Copenhagen, Geneva and Tokyo. On the wage front, Seoul ranked 38th, between Hong Kong and Taipei. Putting these two measures together, Seoul was 42nd in purchasing power based on hourly wages (bracketed by Hong Kong and Tallinn, Estonia).

Seoul is a relatively inexpensive destination for visitors. UBS used a basket of goods comprising a hotel stay, a meal with wine, a rental car, theater tickets, public transportation fare, and a few incidentals to rate the cost of a short stay in major cities worldwide. The total amount for such a trip in Seoul was $630; the worldwide average was $650. Seoul is comparable to such cities as Taipei ($600), Athens ($600), Sydney ($630), Los Angeles ($660) and Chicago ($670). It was far less expensive than Tokyo ($1,130), London ($1,000), Shanghai ($900) and New York ($870). Travelers should take these results with a grain of salt, however, as fluctuations in exchange rates can quickly rearrange the rankings.

THE BIG MAC INDEX

Time it takes for the average Seoulite to earn the money to purchase a Big Mac: 27 minutes (worldwide average: 37 minutes).
- A kilo (2.2 lb.) of bread: 21 minutes (average: 22 minutes).
- A kilo of rice: 20 minutes (average: 25 minutes).
- An 8 GB iPod Nano: 22 hours.

Did you know. . .

that some Korean companies and government agencies have adopted a "wage peak" system for senior employees? Under this system, older workers' salaries are gradually reduced as they approach retirement age in exchange for job security.

Did you know. . .

that rather than lay off workers in the wake of the global recession, Korean companies are typically retaining their workers and some are even hiring? They are doing so as part of a voluntary national strategy in which everyone from production workers to executives agrees to a program of wage and benefits cuts and freezes in order to promote employment.

EDUCATION AT A PRICE

The average Korean household spends about 7.4 percent of its income on education, but this figure rises to over eight percent when the cost of sending children to universities and colleges abroad is included. (There are about 110,000 Koreans studying in the U.S. alone). In Gangnam, one of the wealthiest districts of Seoul, the amount spent on education is staggering. The average monthly household income in Gangnam is 4.8 million won; nearly 1.3 million won of that is spent on education (mainly in the form of private lessons).

South Korean households far outspend their counterparts in other nations on education. In the U.S., household spending on education is 2.6 percent, in Japan 2.2 percent, in Great Britain 1.5 percent and in France 0.8 percent.

Did you know. . .

that in the 1970s the Korean government, in an effort to boost its shipbuilding industry, mandated that all oil transported to Korea had to arrive in Korean-built ships? Korea and China are currently neck-and-neck for the title of the world's largest ship-building nation. With shipbuilding orders down due to the global economic slowdown, major Korean shipbuilders like Hyundai Heavy Industries, Samsung Heavy Industries, and Daewoo Shipbuilding and Marine Engineering are diversifying into the wind power business.

Did you know...

THE FACE OF MONEY

The modern Korean financial system dates to 1950 and the founding of the Bank of Korea. The physical currency is created by the Korea Minting & Security Printing Corporation, which is based in the city of Daejeon, 150 kilometers (93 miles) south of Seoul. The first Korean paper currency was issued in 1402, and was printed on paper made from the mulberry tree.

Numismatists and casual money lovers may be interested in visiting the Bank of Korea Museum in downtown Seoul (museum.bok.or.kr). The museum has displays and hands-on exhibits covering everything from domestic and foreign coins to currency production and the Korean economy.

The following images appear on South Korean currency:

500 won coin: A crane. Cranes traditionally symbolize longevity.

Did you know...

They said it

"Koreans have become increasingly reluctant to work for economic development at the expense of their individual well-being. They are no longer willing to work on Sundays as in the past, and companies have a hard time putting workers on Sunday shifts. Company machinery in the so-called three-D sector—dirty, difficult and dangerous—is often left idle for lack of workers."

– Lee Hyung-koo in his 1996 book *The Korean Economy.*

1,000 won bill: Yi Hwang (1501-1570). Also known as Toegye, Yi Hwang was a renowned Confucian scholar. Well known for his integrity, he took part in several government purges of corrupt officials and was occasionally exiled from Seoul due to his principles. Prior to his death he began constructing the Confucian academy Dosan Seowon, which is portrayed on the bill's reverse side.

5,000 won bill: Yi I (1536-1584). Also known as Yulgok or "Chestnut Valley," Yi I was a child prodigy, a Confucian scholar, and a contemporary of Yi Hwang. Yi I is well known for his writings on Confucian theory, government administration and national defense.

10,000 won bill: King Sejong (1397-1450). Sejong is Korea's best-known king. During his reign numerous advances were made in the arts and sciences, including the development of Hangeul, the Korean alphabet.

50,000 won bill: Shin Saimdang (1504-1551). Shin was an artist, writer and calligrapher; she was also the mother of Yi I (see 5,000 won bill). Shin Saimdang (a pen name) is often referred to as "wise mother" for the prominent role she took in Yi I's education and his growth into a prominent scholar. The 50,000 bill debuted in 2009, and Shin is the first woman to appear on a South Korean banknote. Not everyone, however, was pleased with her selection for the honor; some felt that the choice had anti-feminist overtones in that it suggested women should stay home and devote their lives to their children's education.

Then and Now

Today's Seoul is unrecognizable from what it was 50 or 100 years ago. Many cities in the West have had to cope with decline, but Seoul's biggest challenge in the last few decades has been managing growth. For the average person, life in the capital is better now than it has been at any point in history.

In the 1950s, Seoul struggled to recover from the ravages of the Korean War. It was a poor city, with a ruined infrastructure. Today, South Korea's future oriented capital is an economic powerhouse, and anchors one of the world's most technologically advanced nations. The scope of the changes that have occurred in the last century to the city physically, in day-to-day life, and in Seoulites' way of thinking are truly astonishing, and are a testament to the Korean people's resilience, determination and enterprise.

POPULATION OVER TIME

Seoul's population peaked in the 1990s, and has now stabilized at around 10.5 million people. The population of the capital region, which comprises Seoul, Incheon City and Gyeonggi Province, is more than double the city number, placing Seoul among the world's most populous urban areas. Since the late 1980s, population growth in the capital region has primarily occurred in the outlying areas and satellite cities, rather than in Seoul proper.

1428	109,372 (men aged 16 to 60 only)
1885	197,074
1910	278,958
1926	306,363
1930	355,426
1936	727,241*
1942	1,114,000
1945	901,371
1949	1,418,025
1963	3,254,630*
1970	5,433,198
1976	7,254,958
1988	10,286,503
2006	10,356,202
2008	10,456,034

* City limits expanded

FOREIGN POPULATION

Seoul hosts a growing foreign population. At one time, foreigners were rare in the capital, but now Seoul, like other economically powerful cities worldwide, has developed a thriving international community.

The foreign population reflects Korea's relations with the rest of the world. From the late nineteenth century until 1945, the foreign population was mainly Japanese. In 1926, there were 73,000 Japanese citizens in Seoul and just 500 Americans. Following the Korean War, U.S. citizens dominated the foreign ranks, due to their large military and diplomatic presence. Since the mid-1990s, the rise of China as an economic power has led Chinese nationals to take the top spot in the

They said it

"The sun was just casting his last glorious rays on the horizon, and the excitement grew greater as the strokes of the bell became fainter and fainter, and with the mad crowd of men and beast mixed together upon it, the road might be compared with the tide entering the mouth of a running river."

– Writer, painter and world traveler A. Henry Savage-Landor describing his 1891 entrance into Seoul as the gates were closing. From his 1895 book *Corea or Cho-sen The Land of the Morning Calm.*

foreign population derby.

Seoul's non-Korean residents now total 229,000 and come from a variety of nations. They typically fall under five categories: business people, teachers (usually ESL instructors), military and government personnel, economic migrants and students.

ANCIENT GATES AND WALLS

The city of Seoul was once surrounded by a high stone wall measuring 18.5 kilometers (11.5 miles) in length. Parts of this ancient wall still remain. The northern section between the North Gate (Bukdaemun) and the Gate of Showing Correctness (Changuimun) is outstanding for hiking and popular among nature and history buffs.

The wall was built in the 1390s and incorporates four greater and four lesser gates. Geomancy, or *pungsu-jiri*, which emphasizes the role of the elements and the earth's energy in human life, played a key role in deciding the placement of the gates.

The gates symbolize the four seasons, while also representing the four principles of humanity: benevolence, righteousness, courtesy and wisdom.

Until the late 1890s, the gates of Seoul were shut in the evening and not opened until the following morning. A large bell signaled their closing, and travelers caught outside the gates were stuck. They were either forced to take shelter in one of the villages surrounding Seoul or find a dark and uninhabited part of the wall and climb over.

TAKE5 FIVE MAJOR
HISTORY AND CULTURE MUSEUMS

1. **National Museum of Korea (NMK).** The NMK contains over 200,000 cultural relics and artifacts, and is a sanctuary for over 5,000 years of Korean art, culture and history. The museum's expansive Yongsan complex was completed in 2005, and represents a bold contemporary interpretation of traditional Korean architecture. The NMK and its beautiful grounds are a must for anyone interested in Korean culture. For a list of five of the museum's greatest treasures courtesy of the NMK director, please see the "Timeline" chapter. www.museum.go.kr.

2. **The War Memorial of Korea.** This spacious memorial and museum is located in Yongsan on the former site of the Republic of Korea's army headquarters. It was completed in the 1990s and comprises 9,000 artifacts. These items are displayed indoors and out and range from tanks and helicopters to swords, uniforms and historical documents. The museum, memorial and monuments honor war vets, and provide a valuable education about the history and terrible cost of armed conflict on the Korean Peninsula. www.warmemo.or.kr.

3. **Seoul Museum of History.** Located in the heart of Seoul next to Gyeonghuigung Palace, the Seoul Museum of History provides a wonderful exposition of the city's cultural heritage and development from early Joseon times to present. It also documents the lives of everyday Seoulites in days gone by. museum.seoul.kr.

4. **National Palace Museum of Korea.** Located on the grounds of Gyeongbokgung Palace, the Palace Museum is a treasure trove of Joseon-era artifacts. It illuminates Joseon architecture, culture, arts, science, beliefs and court life in a collection of items ranging from 1392 to 1910. Exhibits include everything from paintings and ceremonial clothing to water clocks and palanquins. www.gogung.go.kr.

5. **The National Folk Museum of Korea (NFMK).** The NFMK is also on the grounds of Gyeongbokgung Palace, and is dedicated to preserving and illuminating traditional Korean life. The NFMK provides a fascinating window onto how ordinary people from centuries ago survived the elements, made a living, worshipped and functioned as families and social units. www.nfm.go.kr.

Did you know. . .

that the Amsa-dong Prehistoric Settlement, which documents and preserves artifacts from life in the Neolithic period, was discovered after a 1925 flood of the Han River? After the deluge, ancient comb-patterned pottery from several millennia ago surfaced, leading to further archeological findings. The site, located in Gangdong-gu on the south side of the Han, was inhabited as long as 5,000 years ago.

GREAT GATES

Bukdaemun (North Gate) also known as Sukjeongmun (Gate of Solemn Rule)

Bukdaemun/Sukjeongmun is unlike Seoul's other major gates in that it was little used in the transport of people or goods. It appears to have been built for geomantic reasons, and was often deployed in an effort to influence the weather (it was opened during times of severe drought). This gate also provided an emergency exit for the royal family, allowing them to escape to the northern fortress located in the mountains directly behind the city. Following the assault by North Korean commandos on the Blue House (the presidential residence) in 1968, the vicinity around the gate was closed to the public. The lovely area is now entirely peaceful, and was reopened to visitors in 2007. A pass, obtainable at www.bukak.or.kr, is required.

Did you know. . .

that at the end of the nineteenth century it was illegal to walk and smoke a pipe in Seoul? Pipes in those days were very long, some almost a meter (3.3 feet) in length, and injuries to the mouth and throat were common from people falling down, or being bumped, while carrying a pipe in their mouth.

The American Empress

In November 1903, readers of the *Boston Sunday Post* were treated to a full-page article entitled, "How the Only American Empress Was Crowned." Half the page was devoted to an ink drawing of a lavish royal wedding procession for Gojong, the Korean monarch, and Emily Brown, a prim and proper American woman.

The story of Gojong's marriage to the daughter of an American missionary was a sensation, and was picked up by newspapers in North America and Europe. According to their accounts, young Emily had accompanied her father to Seoul in early 1894 to assist him in his missionary work. In October 1895, King Gojong was widowed when his wife, Queen Min, was assassinated. Over the next several years, the Korean monarch mourned the loss of his beloved Queen, but one day Emily Brown came to his attention.

Brown had graced her Seoul church choir with her beautiful voice and sparkling character, and apparently had learned to speak fluent Korean in only one year. Gojong soon commanded that she attend him at his palace, but she, a virtuous woman, demurred. Gojong was persistent, and it was only after Brown "obtained the Emperor's promise of marriage at the earliest date," and, according to some sources, his pledge to convert Korea to Christianity, did she agree to enter into his court. Her charm and wisdom won over the palace, and she and the Korean emperor were soon married.

It was a touching and amazing story which had one slight problem: no Emily Brown ever existed. Regardless, for nearly a decade, stories of the fictional Brown and her royal Korean marriage appeared in a variety of publications. Until several years ago, some Internet sites still listed Emily Brown as Gojong's second wife.

The precise origin of this century-old urban legend remains murky. It appears that a foreign newsman in Seoul concocted the story, and the various newspapers that reprinted and commented on the tale never bothered to confirm its veracity.

TAKE5 FIVE TRANSPORTATION FIRSTS

1. **Bicycle (1884).** Philip V. Lansdale, an American naval officer, rides his bike from Incheon to Seoul. Lansdale is also said to have introduced ice skates to Korea.

2. **Train (1899).** A steam-powered train takes passenger between Incheon and Seoul.

3. **Streetcar (1899).** Huge crowds turn out to applaud the first tram. Seoul streetcar service ended in 1968, but six years later the first line of the subway opened.

4. **Bus (1928).** The system debuts with ten buses transporting passengers between Seoul Station and other downtown locations.

5. **Airplane (1913).** A Japanese pilot tests an aircraft near Yongsan military base.

Namdaemun (South Gate) also known as Sungnyemun (Gate of the Exalted Ceremonies)

Namdaemun/Sungnyemun is Seoul's oldest wooden building, and the city's most beloved and well-known gate. It was the main entrance to the city, and Namdaemun Market takes its name from its famous neighbor. During the Korean War, the gate was badly damaged, and in 1961 it underwent extensive repairs. In 1962, it was named National Treasure No. 1. Unfortunately, in February 2008 the upper level of Namdaemun was damaged by an arsonist. The South Korean government is restoring the treasured gate to its former glory; work is scheduled to be completed by the end of 2012.

Did you know. . .

that Korea's first traffic regulations were established in Seoul in 1915? A 1919 law made it illegal to drive with a courtesan in one's car.

Dongdaemun (East Gate) also known as Heunginjimun (Gate of Rising Benevolence)

Dongdaemun/Heunginjimun once served as the primary entrance into Seoul and has been renovated several times, most recently in 1869. The gate has been central to Seoul's modernization and development, and the city's first large electrical power plant was erected nearby in 1899. During the same period, a streetcar line was established and ran through the arch of the gate. Dongdaemun Market was born a few years later; it is now a global center for the clothing and fashion industries.

Colonial Times

The colonial period began in 1910 with Korea's annexation by Japan; it ended in 1945 with Japan's World War II surrender. Prior to the occupation, the Japanese presence was already substantial: Korea was declared a protectorate of Japan in 1905, and there had been several decades of Japanese influence dating to a lopsided 1876 treaty imposed on Korea. Following the 1910 annexation, Hanseong (Seoul) was named colonial capital and given the name Keijo in Japanese, or Gyeongseong in Korean.

In 1910, the Japanese population in Korea was about 171,000, but in only a decade it had doubled to 346,000 and by 1938 it stood at 633,000. Many of these newcomers were farmers who bought great tracts of land from the colonial government.

Most of the large industries and factories were owned by the Japanese, and the majority of technicians and skilled labor were also Japanese. General laborers were mainly Korean, and were typically paid far less than their Japanese counterparts.

Large numbers of Koreans were also sent to Japan, and Japanese-controlled regions, to work in mines and factories and even serve in the military.

Korea's land, resources and people weren't the only things threatened during this period — the Korean language, identity and history were also under attack. In the 1930s, Koreans were

Seodaemun (West Gate) also known as Donuimun (Gate of Loyalty)

Seodaemun/Donuimun fell victim to urban development in 1915. Chinese envoys used to enter Seoul through this gate, but it was closed at one point due to fears that it was interfering with Gyeongbokgung Palace's natural energy. The gate is being reconstructed; work is expected to be completed by 2013.

urged to stop wearing their traditional white clothing, and, in an effort to make Korean students "loyal and obedient" subjects of the Japanese emperor, education was radically reformed.

Most teachers in Korean schools were Japanese, and the study of the Japanese language and history was made compulsory. Although the Korean language was still taught in schools until 1938, Korean history had been removed from the curriculum. Later, Korean students were prohibited from speaking Korean in school (and even at home) at the risk of expulsion. Finally, Koreans were urged to adopt Japanese first and last names, and required to take part in Shinto ceremonies and worship.

Many Koreans resisted the Japanese presence, and there were protests and demonstrations, most famously the nationwide March 1, 1919 independence movement known as the *Samil Undong*. There were also Korean nationalist guerilla groups in China and Russia, and the Provisional Government of Korea in exile was established in Shanghai.

The Japanese occupation represents a dark time in Korean history, but it was also a period during which Seoul and Korea modernized substantially. A number of prominent buildings were constructed during this era, and Seoul's population and footprint expanded significantly.

The Korean War
(and the Years Preceding It)

The Korean War had its origins in the post-World War II partition of Korea into a U.S. occupied zone south of the 38th parallel, and a Soviet zone in the north. In 1948, two separate countries emerged from this division: the Republic of Korea (ROK) in the south, and the communist Democratic People's Republic of Korea in the north (DPRK).

The war itself began on June 25, 1950 when North Korean troops launched a surprise attack, swarming across the border and quickly overrunning most of South Korea. Within three days of the invasion, Seoul had fallen, hundreds of people were killed, and hundreds of thousands trapped in the city when the Han River Bridge was destroyed.

U.N. soldiers from 16 countries intervened, with the U.S. supplying the bulk of the foreign troops fighting alongside ROK soldiers. North Korea received substantial support from China, which provided over 500,000 soldiers during the conflict.

Seoul was recaptured in September 1950 following U.S. General Douglas MacArthur's landing at Incheon, but the victory was only accomplished after heavy bombardment and three days of street fighting. In January 1951, Seoul was again captured by the Communists, but was retaken by U.S./U.N. forces in March.

The war continued for another two years, and an armistice to end the fighting was not signed until July 1953. A border between the two countries was established at the same point it had been prior to the conflict, and a demilitarized zone was demarcated to serve as a buffer.

The cost of the war was horrendous: About one million South Korean civilians were killed, and many times that number rendered homeless. Over 560,000 U.N. and ROK soldiers died, and 1.6 million North Korean and Chinese troops were killed.

Seoul was devastated, but conditions had been difficult even prior to the war's outbreak. Hundreds of thousands of Koreans were repatriated from China and Japan following the end of World

War II. Most of them gravitated to Seoul, where they were joined by refugees from the North. This huge rise in population produced rampant inflation, unemployment and overcrowding. Goods were scarce, and crime surged.

Although Korea was no longer exporting agricultural goods to Japan, Seoulites' diet was affected by problems transporting rice from the countryside to urban areas. Hunger was widespread, and the daily average caloric intake fell by 28 percent from 1936 to 1947.

Many Korean industries failed when the Japanese left. Raw materials were in short supply and there was a lack of skilled technicians and engineers who could repair industrial machinery. Prior to liberation, there were nearly 250 streetcars in Seoul, but by 1947 only 30 were running.

In addition, nearly 95 percent of the South's electrical needs were supplied by dams in the North, but in retaliation for the May 1948 elections establishing the Republic of Korea, the North Koreans cut off the power. The fragile South Korean economy declined further as a result.

By 1949 South Korea was still dependent upon the U.S. for raw materials, industrial replacement parts and petroleum, but it was making substantial improvements in agriculture. The North Korean invasion in June 1950, however, derailed South Korea's development plans.

At the time of the 1953 armistice, Seoul was barely functioning. Entire blocks were flattened, and many of the larger buildings had been reduced to skeletal remains. Few streets were paved, and properly stocked restaurants and shops were found only inside U.S. Army camps.

Hard work, foreign aid and the strength of the Korean family and social structures enabled South Korea to rebuild. Following years of occupation, privation and war, the country drew on its ancient culture and values and fused these with twentieth century know-how. Within decades, South Korea had regenerated itself as a prosperous and democratic nation.

SMALL GATES
Dongsomun (Small East Gate) also known as Hyehwamun (Gate of the Distribution of Loyalty) or Honghwamun

Dongsomun/Hyehwamun/Honghwamun was used by envoys from northern Manchuria to enter the city, but lost much of its importance when Chinese envoys began to use Seodaemun. Torn down in 1928 but reconstructed in 1992, Dongsomun is located in the Daehangno area near Hansung University.

Seosomun (Small West Gate) also known as Souimun (Gate of the Promotion of Justice)

Seosomun/Souimun has a dark past. Prior to the twentieth century, it was one of two "corpse gates" used to remove dead bodies from the city. Moreover, criminals were sometimes executed in the vicinity. It was torn down in 1914.

Gwanghuimun (Gate of Bright Light)

Also once a "corpse gate," Gwanghuimun had the additional title of "floodgate" because of its proximity to Cheonggyecheon Stream. It was restored in 1975, and is located in the Euljiro area of downtown Seoul.

Changuimun (Gate of Showing Correctness) also known as Jahamun (Jaha Valley Gate)

Changuimun/Jahamun is one of the least known gates. It has a unique roof rarely seen on Korean gates, and with the exception of a major

Did you know...

that there were 86 permanent bridges in Seoul in 1910, but only one of them crossed the Han River? A railway bridge traversing the Han was completed in 1900, but Seoul's other bridges of the time crossed the streams and rivers found throughout the city. There are now 24 bridges spanning the Han in Seoul.

1958 restoration, has remained more or less untouched over time. The gate is north of the Blue House, in a pass between Bugaksan Mountain and Inwangsan Mountain. This is a particularly scenic spot to hike the Seoul Fortress walls.

THE RICKSHAW'S RISE AND FALL

Prior to the 1880s, most people got around Seoul on foot. Others rode on horseback, while those of a certain class might be carried through the streets on a palanquin (a small chamber supported by poles and borne by two or more men).

In 1883, a new mode of private transportation, the rickshaw, was introduced. Rickshaws failed to catch on at first, but a dozen years later they returned to the streets of the capital, and by the early twentieth century had become common. Doctors employed them to make house-calls, foreign visitors used them to travel about the city, and the rich and influential flaunted them as status symbols. In the early 1920s, Seoul's several thousand rickshaws were an integral part of the local transportation system, and rickshaw drivers even had their own powerful union.

The human-powered two-wheeled cart's heyday ended in 1912. The automobile taxi had arrived, and cars soon began to compete with rickshaw operators. In 1930, more than half of the private motor vehicles in Korea were taxis, and the number of rickshaws had fallen to fewer than 1,000.

Did you know. . .

that by August 1945, about four million Koreans (roughly 16 percent of the population) were living outside of Korea? Japan, China and Russia were home to many Koreans. Some of these expats were voluntary exiles, while others had been forcibly removed by the Japanese.

THE MOTOR CAR

The automobile made its Korean debut in 1901 when Chicago-born Burton Holmes, a famous lecturer and inventor of the "travelogue," drove his car from Incheon to Seoul.

Members of the Korean royal family in the early twentieth century were the first to own a car. Several foreign businessmen also tooled about Seoul in the early days of the motor car, but cars were very much a rarity. Throughout

TAKE 5 ANDREI LANKOV'S FIVE KEY CHANGES IN POST-WAR SEOUL

Andrei Lankov, Ph.D., was born in St. Petersburg, Russia, and is an Associate Professor at Kookmin University in Seoul. He has written and lectured widely on the history, politics and society of North and South Korea, and is a regular contributor to scholarly journals, as well as to *The New York Times, Asia Times, The Korea Times* and other publications. He is the author of a number of books including The Dawn of Modern Korea, North of the DMZ: Essays on Daily Life in North Korea and *From Stalin to Kim Il Sung: The Formation of North Korea, 1945-1960.*

1. Development of the Gangnam Area
For centuries, Seoul was located on the northern bank of the Han River. The development of the region south of the Han opened the way for southward expansion, and changed the entire geography of the city. It made Seoul into a city of 10 million people, and also made possible its thorough modernization.

2. Building of the Subway
Seoul has one of the best public transportation systems in the world: It is fast, cheap, clean and reliable. The subway, whose first line opened in 1974, is the backbone of this network, and without it the city would be unlivable.

much of the early and mid-twentieth century, private automobiles were comparatively rare in Korea because of an undeveloped transportation infrastructure, the Korean War's impact and a lack of disposable income.

In the 1970s, the growth of a Korean middle class, the strengthening of the road and highway network and the rise of a domestic auto industry paved the way for a Korean car culture. Today, there are more than seven million cars in the greater Seoul metropolitan area alone.

3. The Rise of the Private Automobile

In 1948, there were 10,000 motor vehicles nationwide. Now, there are 17 million. In the 1980s, South Korea became a nation of car owners. This does not necessarily help people commute faster, but it does make travel outside the city convenient.

4. The Rise of Modern Retail

In the 1950s, Seoulites shopped at markets that had changed little since the time of the Joseon Kingdom. Now they shop at department stores (there were four or five in the late 1950s), discount supermarkets (there were none), and convenience stores (appeared in the late 1980s).

5. The Construction of Large-Scale Apartment Blocks

In the late 1950s, nearly all residents of Seoul lived in traditional or semi-traditional houses (beautiful, perhaps, but not very convenient). The switch to high-rise residential complexes, which began with the construction of the Mapo Apartments in 1962, changed Seoulites' lifestyles immensely.

CARS IN SEOUL

1965	16,624
1970	60,442
1980	206,778
1985	445,807
1990	1,193,633
2002	2,691,431 (Greater Metropolitan Area 6,484,000)
2006	2,856,857 (Greater Metropolitan 7,319,000)

TAKE5 ROBERT NEFF'S TOP FIVE
SEOUL GHOST STORIES

Robert D. Neff is a writer and researcher specializing in Korean history. He has written many historical articles appearing in *The Korea Times* and elsewhere, and is author or co-author of the books *Westerners' Lives in Joseon Korea* (2008) and *Korea Through Western Eyes* (2009).

1. Restless Dead in Yongsan
The sprawling U.S. military base in Yongsan is said to be haunted. One building is rumored to have been used as a crematorium during the Japanese colonial era, although there is no evidence to support this claim. Predictably, the restless dead are still said to be making their presence known with fleeting shadows and bumps in the night.

2. Blood on their Hands
In 1921, a popular restaurant in the Nagwon area of central Seoul patronized by Japanese and Korean collaborators was suddenly plagued with vengeful Korean ghosts. Inexplicably, blood would fall on diners and on the restaurant's owner. The police could not solve the mystery, and by year's end the restaurant had lost all its customers. The proprietress was soon driven mad and took to wandering the streets.

SKYSCRAPERS

Contemporary Seoul is a city of towering buildings, but it wasn't always this way. One hundred twenty years ago, Seoul was a walled city of single-story structures. Dwellings were made of wood and tile for the upper classes, and stone and thatch for the lower orders. It was considered a breach of etiquette to be able to peer over one's fence into neighboring courtyards (and especially into the palace), so most buildings in Seoul had one floor.

3. Fleeting Images in Gwangnaru

Since the 1960s, people have claimed to have seen ghosts in this area in eastern Seoul. In the 1990s, there was a strange sighting at the Gwangnaru subway station during the taping of a popular singer's music video. A female ghost was witnessed (and caught on tape) riding in the driver's compartment of a passing subway. The ghost was believed to be that of a young girl who had been murdered at the nearby Han River. The tape has since been dismissed as a hoax, but the rumors persist.

4. Ghost Children

As late as the 1960s, some unmarried Korean women and widows explained their pregnancies as the result of being raped by ghosts. In an attempt to add legitimacy to their claims, they often went to great lengths to try and convince their neighbors that their homes were haunted.

5. **Dongdaemun Spirit Vanquished.** An area near Dongdaemun Market and Gate was said to be particularly haunted until a church was built on the site in the mid-1980s. Prior to the church's construction, the young and inquisitive would visit the area in the early evening; however, once darkness fell, they would flee in fright – their curiosity sated.

There were a few two-story buildings at the end of the nineteenth century, but these were generally built by foreigners. Prominent among the early "tall" buildings were the Russian Legation (1890), the Sontag Hotel (1902) and Myeongdong Cathedral (1898). The Cathedral is still very much in use and remains a Seoul landmark. The Sontag, which was one of Korea's first Western-style hotels (it hosted Winston Churchill among other dignitaries), became a school dormitory and was later torn down. The Russian Legation survives in rump form. In the mid-1890s it was a refuge for King Gojong, who had fled the royal palace in the wake of the Queen's assassination. The legation was bombed during the Korea War, but its tower survives.

During the Japanese colonial period (1910-45), the government built a number of three-to-six-story structures including banks, offices, hotels, and department stores. The most famous remaining colonial-era building is old Seoul Station, which was completed in 1925 in the classically inspired Palladian style.

Following the Korean War, Seoul began to rebuild and modernize. Larger and taller buildings were constructed, although in 1960 there were still no buildings greater than ten stories. All that changed in 1969 when the Samil (March First) Building was completed. Named for the pro-independence demonstration that took place on March 1, 1919, it was a towering 31 stories.

By 1980, there were 25 buildings in Seoul measuring 20 stories or more. In 1985, symbolic of Korea's growing prosperity, the 63-story Daehan Life Insurance Building was completed. At the time, it was

Did you know. . .

that the first computers in Korea arrived in 1967? Three American-built IBM 1401 mainframes and one Japanese-built FACOM 222 were imported for research purposes, and to analyze Korean census data. Korea is now a world leader in the IT sector, and Seoul ranks as the world's most wired city.

the tallest in Asia, and under its current name of 63 City remains a popular tourist attraction.

There is a new wave of tall buildings on the horizon. Currently in varying stages of development, these super skyscrapers will be well over 100 stories and rank among the world's tallest when completed.

HAIR CUTS

In early 1897, haircuts were more than a fashion statement — they carried a political message. As a result of Japanese-backed efforts to reform and modernize Korea, a law was passed requiring all men to have short hair. At the time, top-knots were prized by Korean men, and to be without one was a source of embarrassment and shame.

TAKE5 FIVE FOREIGN FAST FOOD FIRSTS

1. **Coca Cola.** Coke first appeared in Korean stores in 1956, but proved unpopular with Korean consumers and was withdrawn. It returned to stay in 1968.

2. **Kentucky Fried Chicken.** KFC opened its first restaurant in the Jongno area of Seoul in 1984. Kentucky Fried Chicken is one of the most popular foreign chains in South Korea and has dozens of Seoul outlets.

3. **Pizza Hut.** In 1985, Pizza Hut opened its first restaurant in Itaewon. Pizza is popular locally and is similar to Korean food in that a dish placed in the center of the table can be shared by a group.

4. **McDonald's.** The golden arches arrived in Korea in 1988 with the opening of an Apgujeong restaurant.

5. **Dunkin' Donuts and Starbucks**. Dunkin' Donuts debuted in South Korea in 1992 and now has over 700 outlets. Its stores are more stylish and comfortable than those in North America and it has been growing at a fast pace. The first Starbucks opened in 1999 near Seoul's Ewha Woman's University and was an instant success. There are now over 300 Starbucks stores in Korea.

Did you know. . .

As a result, many ignored the government decree, and policemen would snatch long-haired offenders in the streets and shear them of their prized top-knots. Travelers and itinerant merchants from the countryside became afraid to enter the city, and the cost of goods soon rose. Eventually, the government relented and the Korean man was again allowed to wear his top-knot.

This was not the only time that local men have had their locks threatened by the authorities. In the mid-1970s, South Korean police cracked down on long-haired men. The offender was typically marched to a local barber shop under an officer's supervision. Occasionally, the police took matters into their own hands and cut the man's hair right on the spot, or at the police station. This military-inspired practice ended in 1979, but it wasn't until the early 1980s that long-haired Korean males could walk the streets confident that their mane would remain intact.

Did you know. . .

that up until the early 1990s, strong young men were employed as "push men" at some stations of Seoul's subway? During the morning and evening rush hours, the trains were so crowded that it was nearly impossible to close the doors. Push men would gently cram protruding body parts back into the subway cars so that they could be closed. Expansion of the transit network and technological improvements have substantially reduced crowding, ending the "push man" era.

COFFEE

Tea has been a part of Korean life for millennia, but coffee is a relatively recent import. No one is quite sure when coffee was introduced, but more than likely it was in the early 1880s. Coffee was served to foreign visitors at the palace, and King Gojong apparently developed a taste for the beverage himself while staying at the Russian Legation in Seoul in 1896.

In 1898, coffee was used in an assassination attempt on the Korean monarch when a disgruntled former court member slipped poison into Gojong's morning cup. He survived, but the crown prince and chief eunuch fell deathly ill for several days before recovering.

Coffee has now become a part of everyday Korean life. Following the Korean War, casual coffee shops known as *dabang* sprang up. These modest places served a sweet, Korean-style instant coffee, and were common throughout the city. They have now been largely replaced by modern, upscale coffee houses. Most Koreans, however, still rely on instant coffee mixes at home. There are more than 300,000 coffee vending machines in Korea, and Koreans consume 1.8 kilograms (four pounds) of coffee annually per capita.

RADIO

Korea's first regular radio broadcasts began in 1927 when the precursor to the Korean Broadcasting System began operations in Seoul. The newspaper *Chosun Ilbo* had experimented with broadcasting in December 1925, but apparently it did not catch on. South Korea's first private station was established in 1954 by CBS (Christian Broadcast System). In 1966 there were only five major radio stations in South Korea; there are now over 200.

Politics

THE NATIONAL SCENE

"The Miracle on the Han" typically refers to South Korea's rapid post-1960s economic development. The term could also be applied to the country's amazing political evolution.

Following World War II, Korea was freed from Japanese colonial rule and once again became an independent country. It was soon divided, however, into a U.S. controlled zone in the southern part of the Korean Peninsula, and a Soviet controlled area in the north. These zones would later become the Republic of Korea (South Korea), and the Democratic People's Republic of Korea (North Korea).

The two nations fought a three-year-long war that ended in 1953. Following the termination of hostilities, South Korea evolved over several decades into a dynamic and full-fledged democracy. This democratization occurred in tandem with the country's rise as an economic power. In the North, a Communist system has held sway since the 1940s. The standard of living is low, and personal and political freedoms are severely restricted.

The Republic of Korea's first constitution was adopted in 1948. It has since been amended nine times, most recently in 1987. It features a separation of powers between the executive, legislative and judicial branches, and a system of checks and balances.

Seoul is the nation's capital, and the National Assembly Building is located on Yeouido Island in the Han River.

They said it

EXECUTIVE BRANCH
President

The Korean president is the head of state and commander-in-chief of the armed forces. He is elected in a nationwide secret ballot to a non-renewable five-year term. He appoints the prime minister, who must be approved by the National Assembly. Cabinet members, of whom there are between 15 and 30, are appointed by the president on the recommendation of the prime minister. Among other duties, the president grants amnesties, issues decrees to implement laws, and directly supervises the Board of Audit and Inspection, the National Intelligence Service and the Broadcasting and Communications Commission.

The president may not dissolve the National Assembly, and can be impeached for violating the constitution. The prime minister assists the president, and is considered the vice-president of the cabinet. He must be a civilian, and should the president become ill or die, the prime minister may temporarily act in his stead.

Did you know. . .

that Ban Ki-moon's current service as secretary general of the United Nations is not the first time a Korean has played a prominent role at the U.N.? South Korean politician and diplomat Han Seung-soo served as president of the U.N. General Assembly in 2001.

LEGISLATIVE BRANCH
National Assembly
The National Assembly is unicameral and currently has 299 members. Two hundred forty-five are elected by popular vote from individual constituencies, and the remaining 54 are elected by a system of proportional representation. The National Assembly must give its consent to declarations of war, dispatch of troops to foreign nations and granting permission for armed forces from other countries to be stationed on Korean soil.

DISTRIBUTION OF SEATS
Grand National Party (GNP)	169
Democratic Party (DP)	86
Liberty Forward Party (LFP)	17
Pro-Park Alliance (PPA)	8
Democratic Labor Party (DLP)	5
Creative Korea Party (CKP)	2
Solidarity for New Progressive Party (NPP)	1
Unaffiliated	9
Vacant	2

Source: Government of Korea, February 2010

JUDICIAL BRANCH
The chief justice is appointed by the president with the National Assembly's approval, and serves a non-renewable six year term. The chief justice recommends Supreme Court justices, and the president appoints them to renewable six-year terms. In addition to the Supreme Court, there are also High Courts, District Courts, Patent Court, Family Court and Administrative and Local Courts.

Did you know. . .

that the turnout for the 2007 Korean presidential election was near even between the sexes? Men headed to the ballot box at a rate of 63.3 percent, while women turned out at a 63.1 percent clip.

TAKE5 FIVE SIGNIFICANT REPUBLIC OF KOREA
POLITICAL LEADERS

1. Syngman Rhee (1948-1960)
Rhee (1875-1965) was inaugurated as South Korea's first president on August 15, 1948. Decades earlier, Rhee had served as president of the Korean Provisional Government in Shanghai from 1919-1925 when Korea was under Japanese control. Rhee had a strong pro-Western orientation: He converted to Christianity, was educated in the U.S. (including receiving a Ph.D. from Princeton), and lived in the United States for some years, both before and after his presidency. Rhee secured U.S. and U.N. support in resisting the North Korean invasion, a move which proved crucial in enabling South Korea to survive as an independent nation. Rhee was seen by many as a patriot for his resistance to foreign rule, but the Korean War complicated his tenure. He resigned in 1960 in the face of popular opposition to his rule.

2. Park Chung-hee (1963-1979)
Park (1917-1979) is one of South Korea's most important and controversial political figures. During the Korean War, Park was an artillery officer who quickly rose through the ranks and later became a general. In 1961 he led a well-planned coup that toppled the South Korean government. He was elected president in 1963, and left a legacy of economic growth and infrastructure building.

Many of his projects—including the massive steel mills at Pohang and the Seoul-Busan highway—were met with skepticism and deemed impractical. The skeptics were proved wrong. During Park's presidency, per capita yearly income increased from less than $100 to more than $1,000. Unfortunately, he is also remembered for his authoritarian streak, particularly following a 1972 constitutional change that he engineered.

Throughout the 1970s there was much popular opposition to Park's rule, although he was also recognized as a leader in developing the economy. Park was assassinated by the head of the Korean intelligence agency during a private meeting in 1979. His daughter, Park Geun-hye, is a prominent political figure in her own right and a leading member of the Grand National Party.

3. Roh Tae-woo (1988-1993)
Roh (1932-) was the first president since the Republic's 1948 inception to step peacefully into office. That peacefulness, however, was

soon marred by widespread demonstrations. Under Roh's rule, Koreans gained greater liberties and press freedom increased; prior to his election in December 1987 there were 30 daily newspapers, but by the end of 1990 there were 85.

The 1988 Olympics were another highlight of his tenure. South Korea was also opened to foreign markets during this time, a move viewed as a blessing by consumers but perceived as a threat by farmers and manufacturers. Despite his accomplishments, Roh's image was tarnished by bribery allegations and he was eventually imprisoned on corruption and other charges.

4. Kim Young-sam (1993-1998)

Kim (1927-) tried to reform the government through an anti-corruption campaign employing the "Real Name Financial Transaction System." This initiative led to the arrest or resignation of a number of political and military officials. He also further solidified the Republic of Korea as a democratic country whose citizens enjoy a large degree of personal freedom.

During his presidency, amnesty was granted to political prisoners as well as to former presidents Chun Doo-hwan and Roh Tae-woo. Kim also demolished the old Japanese capital building, which had been seen as a painful reminder of colonial rule. The Asian financial crisis occurred during his final year in office, and Kim rallied the Korean people in overcoming this challenge.

5. Kim Dae-jung (1998-2003)

Kim Dae-jung (1925-2009) is famous for his perseverance and ability to overcome opposition. He has been referred to as the Nelson Mandela of Asia, and was a champion of democratization. Kim was arrested several times under the Park Chung-hee and Chun Doo-hwan governments, and was even kidnapped from a Tokyo hotel in 1973 and nearly drowned at sea.

In 1998 Kim was elected president by a very slim margin. His presidency was highlighted by Korea's rapid recovery from the 1997 financial crisis, the success of the 2002 World Cup and the controversial "Sunshine Policy" of engagement with the North. The Sunshine Policy did not pay off as hoped, but Kim remains a crucial figure in the history of the Republic's politics.

The North-South Divide

Since Korea's division into two separate countries in the 1940s, reunification has been a common dream of its people. It is a goal, however, that has proved elusive.

In 1950, North Korea invaded the South and tried to reunify the country through force. U.N. soldiers came to the aid of the South, and the ensuing war ended in a stalemate with a 1953 ceasefire.

The Korean Peninsula's division into two nations is more than an unfortunate political reality and remnant of the Cold War, it has a very human dimension as well. Following World War II, many people were displaced and there are Koreans on both sides of the border who have not seen family members since the 1940s. Over the years there have been family reunions and exchanges, but these have been infrequent, and many Koreans have not had the opportunity to see long lost relatives. Sadly, many of those separated from loved ones are now dying after having lived lives apart.

There have been periodic thaws in the tense relationship, beginning with a breakthrough 1972 meeting which resulted in the North-South joint communiqué. In 1998 Hyundai founder Chung Ju-yung sent 1,001 cattle to North Korea. He also negotiated for South Korean tourist cruises to visit the Mount Geumgang tourist region on North Korea's east coast. More than a million South Korean and foreign guests have since visited the area.

The Gaeseong Industrial Complex, which is located on the North Korean side not far from the DMZ, is another example of closer North-South ties. In early 2009 there were 101 South Korean firms operating at the complex, employing about 39,000 North Koreans. Most of the goods are exported to South Korea, and trade between the two countries in 2008 was about $1.8 billion.

Following talks in June 2000, North and South Korea agreed, among other things, to reconnect their roads and railways at the border. These initiatives helped earn South Korean President Kim Dae-jung, architect of the "Sunshine Policy" of engagement with the North, a Nobel Peace Prize. Finally, in 2007 the railway between Gaeseong in the North and Munsan in the South was connected and a symbolic, rather than commercial, cross-border freight service began. That same year there was another summit between Kim

Jong-il of North Korea and South Korean leader Roh Moo-hyun.

There have also been many provocations, including an attempted raid on the South Korean presidential compound by North Korean commandos in 1968. North Korea's nuclear program also remains a sticking point in closer ties between the two sides. The North has generally been unwilling to allow monitoring of its nuclear activities by international inspectors.

Relations with North Korea are a fault line in South Korean politics: Some advocate keeping the door open to negotiations with the North, even if there are short-term setbacks. Others argue that a program of strings-free engagement by the South with the North, offers of aid, and concessions on the North's nuclear ambitions play into the hands of the unpredictable and bellicose Pyeongyang regime, rewarding a rogue nation for bad behavior.

The matter is also complicated by the U.S. presence in South Korea, and the strategy of employing all six regional players (South Korea, North Korea, the U.S., Japan, China, and Russia) in talks on the peninsula's future.

North Korea remains a mystery. Politicians, academics, journalists and lay people all want to understand its ultimate aims. Are its nuclear activities bargaining chips to be used in negotiations with South Korea and the U.S.? Simply a deterrent against foreign aggression? Or, more darkly, a potential knockout blow to the South and a means of raising cash by selling nukes to other countries? Speculation on the North's intentions runs rife, all the more so given the secretive and apparently unstable nature of the North Korean leadership.

South Korea has made remarkable progress in the last decades, but the matter of North-South reunification, or at least sustained reconciliation, remains unfinished business. While a resolution to this stalemate seems unlikely in the near term, in the case of Germany in the late 1980s, a seemingly intractable divide was erased in but a few short years. Could it happen in Korea? Certainly it wouldn't be any stranger than some of the developments that have occurred on the Korean Peninsula over the last 100 years.

They said it

THE NATIONAL ASSEMBLY BUILDING

Located on Yeouido Island, the green-domed National Assembly is one of Seoul's most recognizable buildings. The National Assembly, whose dome weighs 1,000 metric tonnes, was completed in 1975 and features 24 granite pillars. The octagonal pillars represent the 24 solar terms that divide the year according to the lunisolar calendar. The pillars and dome also symbolize the coming together of the nation's diverse opinions. Parts of the National Assembly are open to tours, and the Visitor Center offers a multi-media exposition on Korean politics (in Korean). The exterior of the Assembly Building is illuminated at night, and surrounded by a large lawn and plaza. In spring, the area's 1,400 blooming cherry trees make it a popular spot for strolling. You can take an animated virtual tour of the Assembly in English at http://korea.assembly.go.kr/vr/main.htm

Did you know...

that Park Chung-hee, South Korean president from 1963-1979, was known for his simple manner and had bricks placed in the toilets of the Blue House to conserve water? The unpretentious Park also favored simple meals like noodles over expensive catered affairs.

They said it

"I've built the road. You build the cars."
— **Former South Korean President Park Chung-hee speaking to Hyundai founder Chung Ju-yung. Park allegedly made the comments after construction was completed on the Gyeongbu Expressway linking Seoul and Busan in 1970.**

PRESIDENT LEE MYUNG-BAK

The Republic of Korea's seventeenth president is Lee Myung-bak of the Grand National Party. He is the tenth person to serve as president since the establishment of the Republic in 1948. A former mayor of Seoul and CEO of the Hyundai Group, Lee was elected in December 2007 on a platform stressing economic growth, closer ties with the U.S. and a tougher stance toward North Korea. One of Lee's most successful initiatives as Seoul mayor was the restoration of Cheonggyecheon Stream. The stream has become a leading tourist attraction and a prime leisure space in the heart of the city.

Lee was born to Korean parents in Osaka, Japan, in 1941 and his family returned to Korea at the end of World War II. Desperately poor as a youth, he went on to serve as head of one of Korea's most powerful conglomerates. In 2009 he followed through on a 2007 campaign promise and gave away much of his personal fortune to a foundation supporting scholarships for needy students. The total amount of the gift was 33 billion won (equivalent at the time to about $26 million).

Did you know. . .

that the main building and two annexes of the Korean president's office are covered in 150,000 traditional blue roof tiles? This is the origin of the "Blue House" moniker for Cheongwadae, the presidential compound. The complex is in northern Seoul and comprises the presidential office, presidential residence and other buildings used for conducting official business and receiving visiting dignitaries.

SEOUL CITY GOVERNMENT

Seoul is divided into 25 autonomous districts or "*gu*," and 522 administrative sub-units known as "*dong*." The "*gu*" execute a number of independent administrative functions, and many would be sizeable cities in their own right. The smallest (Jung-gu) numbers 138,000 residents, while the largest (Songpa-gu) comprises 689,000 people. *Dong* offices function as neighborhood-level providers of city services.

MAYOR'S OFFICE

Seoul mayors have been elected since 1995; prior to that they were appointed. The Seoul mayorship is considered one of the country's most politically powerful positions, and two former mayors have gone on to become president. Yun Bo-seon was appointed mayor of Seoul in 1948, and later served as South Korean president from 1960-62. Lee Myung-bak was elected president of South Korea in 2007 and was Seoul's mayor from 2002-06.

E-GOVERNMENT

Seoul was ranked number one by a wide margin in the U.N.'s 2007 digital governance city survey. The study measured municipal websites on the basis of privacy and security, usability, content, services and citizen participation. Seoul beat out Hong Kong, Helsinki, Singapore and Madrid for the top spot.

Not surprisingly, South Korea also ranked first in the 2010 U.N. Global E-Government Development Index. Korea finished ahead of the U.S., Canada, the U.K. and the Netherlands in a measure which considers e-participation, telecommunications infrastructure, human capital and the content, access and utility of government websites.

Contributing Writers

Mary Crowe has been writing about Korean food since 2003. She blogs at maryeats.com, and her work has appeared in *The Korea Times, The Korea Herald*, the *LUXE Seoul* city guide and *Korea Up Close*. A former resident of Seoul, she now lives in Seattle, Washington, where she is a Marketing and Community Relations Specialist on behalf of Whole Foods Market.

Daniel Gray was born in Daegu, South Korea but adopted by an American family and raised in the United States. After graduating from the University of Delaware, he returned to his native country to teach English and find his birth mother. His love of food and cooking spawned seouleats.com, a blog which has attracted the attention of *The New York Times* and Andrew Zimmern's *Bizarre Foods* program. A Seoul resident since 2004, he is a partner at O'ngo Food Communications, and is working on a Seoul food guide.

Kim Young-sook was born and raised in Seoul. She lived in New York from 1996-2002, and received an M.A. degree in TESOL from the State University of New York, Stony Brook. Since returning to Seoul, she has served as a translator for several leading institutions and companies including the Academy of Korean Studies and Korean Air. She has also acted as a translator, proof reader and copy editor on many children's, educational and technical books, including *Koryeo Dynasty, Bound Treasures* and *Living in Joseon* (I, II, III).

Tim Lehnert has served as editor and contributor on several titles from MacIntyre Purcell Publishing. He is the author of the book *Rhode Island 101*.

Joel Levin is an editor and writer who has held positions with The *JoongAng Daily*, Arirang News, and *Morning Calm* (Korean Air's in-flight magazine). A resident of Seoul since 2002, he has also served as an editorial consultant on behalf of a number of major cultural and historical projects in Seoul, including the Cheonggyecheon stream restoration, the Joseon Kingdom palaces and the National Museum of Korea.

Michael J. Meyers was born in New York but has lived in South Korea since 1980. As Secretary to the Governor of Gyeonggi Province in charge of attracting foreign investment after the 1997 Asian financial crisis, he was South Korea's first foreign civil servant. Mr. Meyers is an English language consultant and a professor of Korean-English/English-Korean translation at Seoul University of Foreign Studies.

Robert D. Neff is a writer and researcher specializing in Korean history. He is particularly interested in Korea's relations with the West from 1880-1910, and Korean gold mines in the 1882-1939 period. He first came to South Korea in 1984 with the U.S. military, and is a long-time Seoul resident. He has written many historical articles appearing in *The Korea Times* and elsewhere, and is author or co-author of the books *Westerners' Lives in Joseon Korea* (2008) and *Korea Through Western Eyes* (2009).

Tracey Stark came to Korea in 2002 after working for several years as a crime reporter for newspapers in North Carolina. He has worked as a sub-editor at the *Korea Herald* and *Yonhap News*, and as an on-air reporter for Arirang Radio. He is currently the editor-in-chief of *Groove Korea* magazine, and a freelance writer and copy editor for several other publications.

Sometimes You Really Can Give Somebody Everything

The editors at the Book of Everything believe that a place is revealed through the accumulation of detail. It is revealed one fact at a time. You find it in variations in weather and climate, pride in favorite sons and daughters, the changing cityscape, local food lingo, and in how people get around, make a living and amuse themselves.

We've made it our job to unearth and marshal those facts so that taken together they reveal a portrait. Books of Everything are not about restaurant and hotel prices, they are books about places and what makes them tick.

MacIntyre Purcell has produced numerous Book of Everything titles including the *Toronto Book of the Everything*, the *Montreal Book of Everything* and the *Vancouver Book of Everything*. There are also Book of Everything volumes on Canadian provinces. In the U.S., MacIntyre Purcell has published similar books on several American states under the 101 series name. For more information, visit www.bookofeverything.com.